HELPMATES

Also by Harry A. Cole

The Long Way Home:
Spiritual Help When Someone You Love
  Has a Stroke

HELPMATES

Support in Times of Critical Illness

Harry A. Cole

Westminster/John Knox Press
Louisville, Kentucky

© 1991 Harry A. Cole

Book design by Gene Harris

First edition

Published by Westminster/John Knox Press
Louisville, Kentucky

PRINTED IN THE UNITED STATES OF AMERICA

9   8   7   6   5   4   3   2

Library of Congress Cataloging-in-Publication Data

Cole, Harry Alexander, 1943–
   Helpmates : support in times of critical illness / Harry A. Cole.
—1st ed.
         p.   cm.
   Includes bibliographical references.
   ISBN 0-664-25141-2

   1. Chronically ill—Home care.   I. Title.
RC108.C64 1991
649.8—dc20   91-15212

To all of the members and each of our friends

of Lochearn Presbyterian Church and

to everyone who cares

Contents

Preface
and Acknowledgments

In the spring of 1987, when my wife and I were guests at the annual conference of the National Head Injury Foundation in Washington, D.C., I met a social worker from Iowa named Janet Cole. After satisfying ourselves that we were not related, and after hearing my story, she suggested that I write a book on spousal support and caregiving in times of critical or chronic illness.

Having committed myself to a writing project earlier that year, it was not until the summer of 1989 that I was able actually to consider writing about what is involved in caring for a sick or injured spouse on a long-term basis. While I knew from my own experience that many husbands and wives are caregiving spouses, I learned that there was very little in the way of practical guidance or suggestions to help them in their caregiving efforts.

For that reason I wrote this book. It is about what we do and how we can do it better, for ourselves and for those whom we love and care for as our life partners. Many of the book's suggestions come from the insight and experiences of caregiving spouses throughout the country whom I interviewed and with whom I corresponded in the course of my research. Truly, this has been a cooperative effort.

I am indebted to those caregivers and everyone else whose cooperation and support has made this book possible, including:

The officials of the American Medical Association and other national organizations who saw the merit of the book and encouraged its writing, especially James J. Lannon, President of the National Stroke Association.

The physicians, nurses, and other members of the medical and helping professions whose contributions to this work provided a unique and invaluable perspective to the caregiving process.

The many program coordinators and support group leaders throughout the country who allowed and arranged for my incursion into the lives of caregiving spouses long enough to learn about their individual experiences and share them with others.

Tad Pula, M.D., for his encouragement in my work and for his clarification of the medical terminology and procedures that are included here as part of the caregiving process.

My agent, Elizabeth Kaplan, of Sterling Lord Literistics, for her interest and support in this project and for the certainty she had that it would become a book.

Louise Bailey and Kelly Valentine-Beam for the typing and printing of the manuscript throughout its successive drafts.

My own helpmate and wife, Jacqueline, who assisted me in the writing process by making corrections and suggestions to improve the manuscript.

My editor at Westminster/John Knox Press, Harold Twiss, for his literary insight, editorial oversight, and patience in helping to bring the book to its final form.

This book is written in special dedication to those I know who love and care: Evelyn, John, Bob, and Frances.

And it is written in special memory of those who were cared for and are still loved: Elva, Debbie, and Bill.

H. A. C.

Introduction

What does a wife do when her husband suffers a sudden heart attack? How does she learn to cope with his condition once it has stabilized and he is released from the hospital? Where does a husband go for help, for himself as well as his wife, when it is discovered that she has breast cancer? What can a husband or wife do to begin rebuilding a marriage after his or her spouse has sustained a serious injury in an automobile accident and faces months and even years of chronic pain and rehabilitation?

Every year thousands of married couples face the consequences of critical illness from cancer, stroke, and heart disease, from neurological disorders ranging from depression to dementia, from serious physical injury, and more. The American Cancer Society states that one million people will fall victim to one or another malignancy in 1992. The American Heart Association predicts that one and one half million people will suffer a heart attack. The National Stroke Association says that one half million people will suffer a stroke, and the Alzheimer's Disease and Related Disorders Association claims that over four million people in this country alone are currently affected by some type of progressively dementing illness. How do medical catastrophes like these affect a couple's relationship?

Critical illness is an unwelcome partner in many more

marriages and intimate personal relationships than we realize. It is no respecter of age, sex, or socioeconomic status. The National Head Injury Foundation reports that two thirds of all serious head injuries occur in persons under thirty-five years of age. According to the American Heart Association, men suffer from cardiovascular disease at a higher rate than women. The American Cancer Society notes that women are biologically more prone to developing breast cancer than men and are developing lung cancer faster due to various changes in their life-styles, which includes increased smoking. The National Center for Health Statistics estimates that over nine million people in the United States are either mentally or physically impaired to the extent that they cannot perform the tasks expected of them. If they are full-time students they cannot adequately learn; if they are home-makers they cannot manage the household; if they seek gainful employment they cannot hold down a responsible job. What does this do to a marriage?

These national organizations study the causes and effects that particular illnesses have on their victims. They document just how widespread the incidence of critical and chronic illness is in our society today and make the case for effective caregiving abundantly clear. Add to this three facts—that medical technology continues to advance in its treatment of catastrophic illness through shock trauma centers and critical care centers in hospitals across the country, that new drugs and surgical procedures are saving literally thousands of lives that would have been lost only a decade ago, and that people are now living longer and are thus more prone to accidents and disease—and the need for improved techniques in long-term caregiving becomes all the more apparent.

In the midst of these impressive developments, however, physicians, nurses, social workers, and other members of the helping and healing professions have begun to realize a sobering truth. Faced with the task of providing for a dependent loved one, caregivers are often unprepared to cope with the myriad of physical and emotional effects that accompany long-term illness. They are simply overwhelmed by their responsibilities. Take for example a husband who has suffered a stroke or heart attack and after the acute phase of his treatment is discharged from the hospital with a home health-care plan that is vital to his recuperation. Following that plan falls to his wife, who lacks both the ability and experience to handle successfully her new role as caregiver. Her husband may have a complicated medication program she cannot understand, and she is afraid to ask the cardiologist to explain it again. He may require help with walking, getting in and out of bed, or toileting himself, and she is physically unable to lift him out of the bathtub or help him up off the floor if he has a fall. He may have a number of emotional issues to confront such as anger, depression, self-doubt, or pity, and the caregiving wife must try to help him resolve these feelings even as she begins to experience them herself. In addition to these responsibilities, with all their attendant complications, the caregiving wife may be forced to assume other such duties such as learning to be a single parent, finding full-time employment, and managing the family budget. She will have to adjust to the role of head of the household while facing a future marked by confusion, uncertainty, and fear.

Under these stressful and often terrifying circumstances, the caregiving spouse is expected to be willing, able, and constantly available to respond to the needs and demands of a husband or wife who may be housebound, bedridden, and totally dependent on someone else for help. It is certain that under these circumstances caregivers need help themselves and cannot do the job that lies before them without adequate guidance, direction, and support.

Within the past few years I have become a caregiving husband as a result of my wife's stroke. In the course of her illness and recovery I have had the opportunity to meet with many other persons who have found themselves in similar situations of caring for their husbands, wives, and other loved ones suffering from critical and chronic illness. As I have come to know these other caregivers, I have found that while each of us is often at a loose or even a dead end in deciding what is best for our loved ones as well as ourselves, ours is a common task that needs to be shared if we are going to do it well. To care for a chronically ill husband or wife on a full- or even a part-time basis with perhaps no end to the task in sight is an act of love and courage that is as physically exhausting and emotionally draining as it is noble in character. Critical illness and disease remain as unwelcome yet persistent partners in our way of life today, and having to suffer from their acute and long-term effects can be an ordeal of major proportions for caregiver and caretaker alike. To care for a loved one who is critically or chronically ill is a major challenge is a person's life, requiring unique skills along with immense patience and dedication.

If we are to rise to the occasion of providing spousal support during periods of critical and chronic illness, we must first realize that we are not alone. Many of us are caregiving spouses, and unfortunately our numbers are increasing. Yet if we are to do our jobs well we should also realize that caring for someone whose personal well-being may totally depend on us presents us with a singular opportunity to discover our capacity for loving another person while learning about our strengths and weaknesses and the values that shape our lives. It is a time for intense, albeit painful, self-encounter and growth, during which we help our loved ones to grow with us in the face of great adversity—which, as I believe from my own experience, is the only time when real growth occurs.

The chances are, if you have picked up this book and read this far, you or someone you know is caring for a husband or wife who has fallen victim to some type of illness or chronic health problem. The person may have had a heart attack, stroke, or sustained a serious physical injury. He or she may be mentally ill or struggling to live with the effects of cancer, Alzheimer's disease, AIDS, or substance abuse such as alcoholism or drug addiction. If you are a caregiving spouse, this book is for you. It will not automatically make your job easier. It will not tell you that if you apply your caregiving efforts long and hard enough, with all the faith and perseverance you can muster, your husband or wife will inevitably recover from whatever illness or disease he or she is suffering from and your job will finally be over. What this book will give you are the information and the practical advice necessary under your special circumstances to do your job as best you can with a greater degree of insight, patience, and understanding. It will also help you realize that while you may be in for the long haul as a caregiving spouse there is always hope, and as you learn to live with your spouse's critical or chronic illness you may also learn from it along the way. Beyond that, this book is for you because it is about people *like* you—people who look for meaning and inspiration in the critical events of their lives, people who care for those they love and who know what you are going through and care about you as well.

1

The Critical Event: A Confirmed Diagnosis

On Saturday, March 29, 1986, the day before Easter, my wife, Jacqueline, suffered a sudden and massive stroke. Her attending physician at the hospital where she was taken for emergency treatment diagnosed its cause as an intercerebral hemorrhage and told us that her condition was so critical she would not live out the day.

It is an obvious understatement to say that here was an incident in my life and the lives of our children for which none of us was even remotely prepared. Jackie was forty-three years old, in seemingly perfect health, engaged in a full-time career, happily involved in the lives of her family and friends, with a bright outlook and great expectations for the future. Suddenly, within a period of minutes, all that changed forever. She complained of a terrible headache and a numbness on her right side, slumped to the floor, and lost consciousness. We called the 911 emergency number and rushed Jackie to the nearest hospital, where she lay in a coma for the next forty-seven days.

What happens when your spouse is suddenly stricken with a life-threatening illness? How do you react to news of imminent death and adjust to the reality of sudden loss and permanent change in your life?

It's a bright warm January afternoon in southern Florida. The sun is shining through the window of a hospital room where Stephen and Louise, recently returned from up north, are waiting for the results of the tests Stephen has undergone the previous day. They make small talk about what they plan to do after they speak with the doctor and then grasp hands as they hear footsteps coming down the hall to their room. The urologist, an older man who has been through this many times before, greets them with a slight smile and then says, gently but firmly, "I'm sorry, but the results of the tests indicate cancer in the prostate. It's too advanced for surgery, but we are going to recommend radiation and estrogen therapy as a method of treatment."

How does this couple absorb the impact of such a diagnosis? How can they begin to face a future that no longer accommodates their plans but instead requires them to center their existence around a lifelong and eventually fatal disease?

Larry and Jennifer are newly married. Larry is just beginning a career in computer sales and uses a small motorcycle to make his calls. One day a car runs a light at an intersection, knocking Larry off the motorcycle and into the path of an oncoming car. As a result of the accident, and even though he wore a protective helmet, Larry is now a quadriplegic. According to his neurologist's prognosis, even after extensive physical therapy he is likely to remain so for the rest of his life.

With her whole life in front of her, Jennifer finds herself in the position of caregiver for her permanently disabled husband. How can she face such a responsibility? What will be required of her? What will she require if she is to face up to the task of caring for Larry for the rest of their lives together?

The onset of critical and chronic illness from injury or disease is perhaps the most devastating event that can occur within a marriage relationship. It can break the bond of unity that sanctifies it. It can destroy the balance of responsibility and level of trust that may have taken years of intense effort and mutual understanding to establish, or it may prevent love and trust from ever developing at all. It can threaten the security and future of the relationship itself by creating havoc and chaos, fear and despair. Critical and chronic illness can change everything in our married lives and threaten us with the loss of our identity as husband, wife, lover, and friend.

Getting bad news in the form of a conclusive diagnosis of a critical or chronic illness is something for which we are never fully prepared or ready to accept. Whether it confirms our worst fears or comes as a complete surprise, we are rarely able to do anything that is immediately helpful. In the moments after the doctors confirmed Jackie's stroke I was confronted with a totally foreign situation. I had no idea of how to respond. There were questions to ask about her diagnosis that I had yet to think of, decisions about her course of treatment I was ill-prepared to make, and advice from physicians and nurses I was unable to comprehend. I felt completely disoriented from the reality of the events unfolding before me and was incapable of responding to any of them.

Many of the couples I spoke to within the course of my interviews recalled reactions to what their physicians told them about a spouse's critical illness with similar feelings of shock, confusion, fear, anger, and denial. If you share in these feelings now that you and your spouse have received bad news from your doctor, you are not alone in your situation. Listen to how a wife from Indiana describes her reaction to her husband's stroke:

> My husband had abdominal surgery. Then he had a stroke right in his room while his doctor was standing beside his bed. I was devastated and I'm still in a state of shock. It was all so sudden.

It's one thing to hear what the doctor is saying about your spouse's stroke. It is quite another to be there while it is actually happening. And this situation was compounded by the fact that the victim's wife thought the medical crisis had passed after successful surgery. Can we imagine her reaction as she realizes that her husband's primary illness is now not only acute but life-threatening? Her claim of personal devastation is quite plausible under these circumstances.

Another caregiving wife spoke from California of her reaction to her husband's illness in this way:

> I cried for two weeks after we found out about my husband's tumor. It was in his brain and we couldn't do anything about it. I would get furious and then I'd feel very helpless and terror-stricken over what was happening, and going to happen, to all of us.

Anger and helplessness are natural responses to occurrences of critical illness. To watch someone we love suffer for no apparent reason while we can do nothing to relieve the pain is an experience of mounting frustration for husbands and wives who, enraged and in tears, come face to face with an emotional abyss in their lives where nothing seems certain or secure any longer. The panic that ensues in reaction to critical illness can cause us to question our very existence and makes us realize how little control we have over our lives and how quickly we can become very much alone.

The husband of a suspected cancer victim reported on his feelings about denying the existence of her illness:

> My wife's cancer was diagnosed during exploratory surgery, so it was not a complete shock. Still, there's no time to prepare for that kind of news. After the doctor left I was numb and kept saying that I couldn't believe we were going through this. Then I got nauseous.

Time and again people have told me that even when they suspected something was seriously wrong with their health they were never quite ready to accept the truth once it was told to them. It is one thing to anticipate bad news about our health; it is quite another to actually hear it. At this point all the mental and emotional preparations that we make to deal with the onset of a critical illness begin to break down. In the case of some caregivers it is an experience that can make them literally sick as well.

A husband whose wife has multiple sclerosis told me:

> At the time my wife was diagnosed I had no idea what to expect. She was still walking and doing housework. But then she met a woman with MS who had lost her ability to talk. My wife was shocked, but I had insulated myself to the point where I had very little emotional response. I just didn't want to believe any of it.

How *can* we believe it—until it happens to us? This is a fair question for anyone who has suffered from a critical illness or disease or has experienced it in the life of someone else. Avoidance and denial are natural responses to events that threaten the routine and security of our lives. For those of us who are caregivers this question is especially relevant; not only must we work through our own denial and begin to accept what has happened to our spouses, we must also help them cope with the reality of their condition as they try to find their own answers to what happened to them and why—answers that in many cases they must literally learn to live with.

News of a debilitating or life-threatening illness strikes at the heart of a marriage relationship. Couples who "pledge their troth" to one another and take each other in "sickness and in health" realize all too quickly what it means to be true to their wedding vows and face the fact that these are not empty words. Pain and suffering are an unwelcome part of any marriage. In the diagnosis of serious illness or disease, caregiving husbands and wives will discover the depth of their commitment to their stricken marriage partner, and to their stricken marriage as well.

2

Coping with Your Feelings

The diagnosis has been confirmed. You know what is wrong. Your spouse has been declared "officially sick" by your family doctor or by a staff physician at your hospital or medical clinic. If you suspected something was wrong, the diagnosis may not have come as a complete shock. It may be a relief because it confirms your suspicions about the severity of your spouse's condition. You may even feel good about yourself because you were right all along—before the doctors were. And now that you are sure of what's wrong, you can breathe a little easier and as a caregiver begin to put things into a workable perspective.

Bad news, however, whether or not it confirms your fears that something is seriously wrong with your spouse's health, is never fully expected. Under the worst of circumstances it is only human for you to hope for a complete recovery, even if it would take a miracle. To claim that the discovery of serious illness or disease holds no element of surprise is to deny the gravity of your spouse's medical condition, and denial can lead to serious consequences—for you as a caregiver as well as for your spouse.

Shock, in fact, is a very real part of your initial reaction to your mate's critical illness. Like the husbands and wives in chapter 1, when you get bad news from the doctor you enter a state of shock, ranging from mild to severe, which provokes some immediate emotional reactions to your partner's illness. These reactions form a process, a coping mechanism for you to use, as you begin to face the various implications of this critical or chronic illness and as you work on your new responsibility of becoming a caregiving spouse. In this chapter we will look more closely at the coping process that caregivers experience after the diagnosis of a spouse's illness has been confirmed.

Much has been written to help us understand our emotions when we react to a crisis event in our lives. You have probably heard about or even experienced the "fight or flight" response, in which you either confront a crisis in your life in order to defeat it or flee in order to avoid it. You may have also experienced anticipatory grief, in which you mourn for the loss of something or someone due to a critical event or illness that has yet to run its course.

Most of the current literature dealing with sudden loss or change in our lives, especially as it relates to illness and disease, can be traced back to the pioneering work with the terminally ill done by the Swiss psychiatrist Elisabeth Kubler-Ross. In her book *On Death and Dying*, published in 1969, Kubler-Ross was the first to recognize that the feelings we experience in reaction to the news of sudden or terminal illness follow a logical progression to form a process of grief in which we gradually learn to cope with and eventually overcome its crippling emotional effects. She identified these feelings as denial, anger, bargaining, depression, and acceptance and investigated their effects in situations where the death of a loved one is imminent. We have come to realize over the last two decades that these same feelings can be expressed in any grief situation and are especially relevant to coping with the basic shock of critical and chronic illness.

These feelings—or stages of grief, as Kubler-Ross defines them—may be familiar to you as a caregiver. You

may have already experienced them in caring for your
husband or wife. You may be going through the process
now. Either way you know that these feelings are not
pleasant and some are very painful. They are often re-
peated as you move from one stage to another and back
again. Some are felt more deeply than others and most
of them will occur in varying degrees throughout the
course of your spouse's illness. But as you initially react
to the shock of your spouse's illness or disease, however
suddenly it comes into your lives, bear in mind that your
feelings are both necessary and natural. They are a natural expression of your loving concern and the need you
have for your husband or wife to get well. They are also
a necessary part of the grieving process that will eventually help you "get well" also. Let's look at the process in
its separate stages more closely.

Denial

When you first get bad news about your loved one's
health you don't want to believe it. And why should you?
It's only natural that you would choose not to listen to all
of what the doctor is saying or what the test results have
revealed. No one likes to hear the worst.

Denial is the total opposite of acceptance. It wants
nothing to do with reality. Denial as the first stage of your
initial reaction to critical illness is appropriate, however,
because it protects you from the full assault of the effects
of your spouse's illness on your own personal security and
well-being. It allows you the opportunity to diminish the
shock of the critical moment so you will not cave in under
the weight of the disaster that has suddenly befallen you.

When I first learned of Jackie's stroke, I refused to
believe it happened. I couldn't; the full impact of that
terrible news would have overwhelmed me. I wanted to
survive, to prevail, and to do that I needed to believe that
Jackie would be fine in order to fuel my attempt to re-

cover from the initial blow and make my life normal again. My denial of the severity of my wife's condition allowed me to do that—it staved off some of the sheer terror and deep sorrow of the moment and put my whole emotional state into neutral long enough for me to gain some distance from the initial shock of her illness.

If you have received bad news about the health of your loved one, you know what it is like to want to deny it. You want to pull the wool over your eyes or stick your head in the sand and pretend that it will go away or that it never happened. It doesn't go away, of course, and it did really happen, but remember: it's *normal* to think otherwise. Self-deception at this point contributes to self-preservation, which is always healthy, but especially so in these circumstances because you, as a caregiver, must learn to prevail if you are going to be of any help to your partner in the future.

Denial, however, has its obvious limitations. To deny the existence or the seriousness of a particular illness can be a dangerous and sometimes fatal coping mechanism. I met a husband and wife at a Christmas party a few years ago, both of whom had denied the existence of her breast cancer for the previous three years. She had been a professional model and could not face the idea of a mastectomy. Her husband had supported her decision to go against her oncologist's advice and choose a less radical form of treatment throughout her illness. Three weeks into the new year she entered the hospital for platinum therapy for her condition, and two weeks later she was dead.

Serious illness rarely cares for its victim. That is where you come in. While you do need to preserve your own physical and mental well-being under the circumstances, your priority will be to care for your spouse. Remember, do not deny the facts of the matter so strongly that you lose your capacity to feel or your ability to act. Don't lose your perspective. You need to begin to confront the reality of what has happened in order to be of significant help, even if that means facing up to the truth and getting very angry.

Anger

Anger is the next stage in the process of coping with serious illness. Once denial serves its purpose and you realize it is useless to continue avoiding the gravity of your spouse's medical condition, you are likely to get angry. Something very wrong has happened to someone you love very much. It is not your spouse's fault or yours and there is nothing either of you can do about it. Maybe no one can. Should you get angry? You bet you should. It is a natural and healthy response for anyone who feels helpless and victimized by circumstances beyond one's control, and in these circumstances you and your spouse will certainly feel both.

Many people are afraid to show their anger, fearing their emotional outbursts will lead to irreparably harmful consequences. Perhaps you are like that—believing that getting mad about your spouse's illness will only make matters worse for both of you. You feel that you will disrupt the routine of your life even more sharply if you get angry; you will alienate the doctors; worst of all, you will aggravate your spouse's condition. Don't believe it. Getting angry about your partner's illness is not the problem. The problem is staying angry and making matters worse. Confronting and expressing your negative emotions about what has happened to your spouse is a necessary part of becoming an effective caregiver.

Over the years I have advised people in crisis situations to give themselves permission to be a little crazy—to behave out of the ordinary on occasion because they have found themselves in extraordinary circumstances. You may agree with a sign I once saw in a doctor's office: "I'm going to have a nervous breakdown today because I've earned it!" So get angry. You've earned it. Acknowledge your feelings. Talk them out with a trusted friend, the hospital chaplain, your own clergyperson, an understanding doctor or nurse, or even a mental health professional if necessary. You may yell, scream, curse, and cry. You may express your deepest feelings of resentment over this terrible intrusion into your married life. You may blame God for causing it and berate the doctors for telling you about it. You may swear up and down that your husband or wife can get well and demand that if no one else will find a cure for this illness you are going to do it yourself. You may even get very angry at your husband or wife for ruining your life by getting sick in the first place. You may do a lot of things that do not make sense, but remember, getting angry at the news of your spouse's critical illness does not need to make sense to anyone except you.

Bargaining

Bargaining is your first rational response to the news of your spouse's critical illness. It is more than an emotional reaction; it evolves out of denial and anger and requires you to make a realistic appraisal of your partner's medical situation and to assess what you can do to contribute to her or his recovery. Bargaining is the first reasonable indication of your commitment to care. It is not so much reactive as it is *proactive.* You want to negotiate for a return of your mate's health.

How hard you bargain and with whom depends on the severity of the illness. If it is a chronic condition like diabetes you will want to engage your husband or wife with an offer to provide care indefinitely if he or she will follow diet and medication instructions. That deal being struck, everything will seem okay with you, even though your spouse is still suffering from the effects of the illness. If the illness is a life-threatening matter, such as a massive heart attack or colon cancer, you will immediately throw patient-spouse responsibility out the window and make

your case with the physicians, with God, or with whatever other healing power you can find. As a caregiver,
you will do anything within your power to assure that
your partner's life will be spared. When I was told that
my wife would not survive her stroke on the day she had
it, I implored the doctors to do everything they could to
save her and assured them that I would do anything to
help. Failing that, I spent several hours that night asking
God to heal Jackie, in exchange for which I would do
anything God asked. I waited all night for a response to
my overture, and even as dawn arrived and nothing was
forthcoming, I was still willing to talk.

The fallacy in this whole scenario, of course, is that I
was in no position to bargain. Bargaining is a rational
response to an irrational situation: critical or chronic illness. In your own case, your best intentions to negotiate
a settlement cannot begin to heal an ailment that may
have taken years to develop and may have no cure in
either the long or the short run. Your husband or wife is
sick and there is very little you can do about it at the
moment except to face up to your situation, which presents a very depressing prospect for your ability to cope
with the reality of your spouse's illness in the future.

Depression

You tried to bargain and it did not work. The situation
has not improved; maybe it has gotten worse. So as reality sets in and you become more resigned to living with
your spouse's illness, you enter the fourth stage of the
coping process: depression and despair.

Some mental health authorities claim that depression
is little more than anger turned inward, which suggests
that if you become depressed about your wife's illness,
for example, you are really angry at yourself for lacking
the ability to make her well. It could be argued, then,
whether depression is really a coping mechanism at all.
You feel increasingly helpless to do anything positive in

a critical illness situation in which improvement seems increasingly doubtful. If you have ever felt this way over your spouse's situation, you know what depression is.

This stage of dealing with critical illness can be the most difficult to get through. Caregivers have admitted to being overwhelmed by the full impact of their spouse's illness. A caregiving husband described his depressive reaction to his wife's cancer this way:

> One morning I woke up and it hit me. I couldn't go to the hospital that day to see her. I couldn't even get out of bed. All of my strength and resolve to help her was gone. For the first time I began to feel that I was going to lose her and there was nothing I could do to change that.

Depression can become chronic in itself for caregivers who, formerly convinced that they could simply demand a cure for their husbands and wives, now believe there is nothing they can do to help them through their ordeal. At this level, depression can immobilize a caregiver's efforts and will probably require professional help to relieve its crippling effects. If you have become depressed to the degree that *you* feel disabled by your mate's illness, if you no longer believe or even care about helping your mate get well, by all means get help for yourself as quickly as possible. You have a job to do, and as depressing as that may sound it is still, unfortunately, the truth.

If depression has any practical application at all as a coping mechanism, it may well serve as a transitional stage in which your personal expectations as a caregiver are lowered to a more realistic level. Depression and despair are sobering experiences and will no doubt lead you to a more practical approach to caring for your husband or wife. As you emerge from your depressed state and realize that you no longer can or need to bear the full responsibility for this illness, you begin to search for acceptable ways that actually help your stricken spouse get well. You move on to a new stage of coping.

Acceptance

After denying the facts of your spouse's medical situation and then fighting against the truth, after failing to negotiate a plan for a speedy return to health, and then feeling overcome by the grim reality of your husband or wife's condition, you reach the last stage of the coping process—you come to accept your partner's illness for what it is: disabling, long-term, or terminal. You realize that the best way—the only way— to deal effectively with it is to learn to accommodate the illness within your lives together.

This act of acceptance, however, need not be passive, nor must it necessarily signal defeat. Again, this is a proactive response, not a reactive one. It may be that neither you nor your spouse will conquer the illness or disease in the short term. It may become chronic; it may be fatal. But in learning to accept the reality of your spouse's illness, along with your own limitations as a caregiver, you will discover what you can do to make the ordeal more bearable for each of you.

A woman from California told me how she came to terms with her husband's stroke.

> After Lou got out of the hospital I was very anxious that he recover completely, and I did all I could to encourage him in that direction. I had heard about other people getting over stroke, even at our age. But coming to the center and seeing all these people who were permanently disabled, I began to realize that Lou might be just like them for the rest of his life. It's taken me a long time to accept that, and even now I still get angry when I think too much about the good old days.

The middle-aged wife of an amiotrophic lateral sclerosis (ALS) patient said this about accepting her husband's illness:

It was so grossly unfair. I know that part of me will never get over watching him falling apart like this. The truth is, though, that the worse he gets the less chance we have for a life together. So I try to accept that and use the time we have now to our best advantage.

Accepting your partner's illness is not giving in to it. Admitting your limitations does not turn you into a quitter or a failure. You are still the same person, the same loving husband or wife who is now able to make an objective analysis of what you can and cannot do to contribute to your spouse's return to health. Recognize this as a positive step in your coping process and the ongoing process of care. Accept what is and fight for what can be. Both you and your spouse will benefit from your insight and courage.

3

Gaining a Workable Perspective

You have been given the news that your spouse is very sick. Once the shock has run its course, whether that takes an hour, a day, a week, or more, you now realize that, except for the attending physician, you bear the primary responsibility for helping your husband or wife through this ordeal.

How do you sort out that responsibility? Where do you go from here?

The late existentialist philosopher and theologian Paul Tillich once observed that creation and chaos go together. In the case of critical and chronic illness this could well mean that out of the confusion and emotional chaos that was part of your initial response to what happened to your spouse, a certain creative force emerges that will allow you, in your unique position as a caregiver, to understand as much as possible about the various dimensions of the illness. You begin by questioning the nature and cause of the illness or disease itself. How will it affect your lives together, now and in the future? What can you do to help your partner recover? And how will the illness or disease resolve itself?

Knowing at least some of the answers to these questions at the start of your caregiving duties will help put your spouse's illness into what chapter 2 called a workable perspective. This is absolutely essential if your caregiving efforts are to be at all effective.

The Illness Event and Its Implications

Your husband has had a heart attack. You know he will be laid up for many weeks, during which time he will depend on you for almost everything. Or your wife has multiple sclerosis. You understand it is a chronic disease whose effects vary in no predictable pattern, but there is no cure and it will never get any better. Beyond a few facts like these, what else do you know about your spouse's condition and what it will all mean to you?

Part of your working perspective requires a rudimentary knowledge of the particular illness or disease. While chapter 4 will be devoted to building a working relationship with the medical team, let me say here that part of what you need to know can be obtained by asking questions of your spouse's doctors, nurses, therapists, or anyone who can give you useful medical information. Beyond that you can learn much about your spouse's illness on your own. Read as much as you can about its causes and effects. Public libraries and patient libraries in hospitals are good sources for the layperson, as are the professional books and medical journals written about specific diseases and their treatments. Newsletters from groups such as the National Stroke Association, the American Cancer Society, and the American Heart Association contain helpful articles and information on personal experiences with these illnesses and diseases.

Talking with other caregivers and patients will prove immensely beneficial. No one knows what it is like to fill your shoes as a caregiver other than those who have already walked in them. Seek out those with similar experiences, such as fellow stroke or heart attack victims and their caregivers. Listen to their stories; learn about the causes and effects of a critical illness or disease in their lives and apply it to your own situation. Ask them questions; they are the true experts. In my experience, they will be only too happy to talk with you because they share your problems. Where do you find such people?

Fortunately for you, they are almost everywhere. You need not join a formal organization or support group at this point to meet them. You can talk to your family physician about a referral; you can ask the hospital chaplain, social worker, or your local pastor for the names of people who would be willing to talk with you.

Meeting your spouse's illness or disease head on by learning as much about it as you can is a courageous and often hard thing to do. You will hear things you wish you hadn't and learn things you wish you did not know. But it is necessary. You need to know as much about the physical dimensions of your spouse's illness as possible. In this case, ignorance is not bliss and knowledge is power.

As you learn about your spouse's illness, you will begin to wonder what it all means to your relationship. How will the illness or disease affect your lives as a married couple now and in the future?

Whatever physical and emotional consequences your spouse suffers as a result of the illness, one thing will become crystal clear: whether permanent or temporary, progressive or sudden, your husband or wife has suffered a major loss. He or she has lost mobility, independence, and self-esteem. He or she may lose a job, friends, and a place in the community. You may both lose a great deal of money in paying uninsured medical expenses. To be ready to sustain these kinds of losses is first to anticipate them. You cannot fully prepare for these costs until they occur, but you can plan on their eventuality and devise a way to lessen their impact.

One loss that will have special meaning to you as a caregiver is your partner's place in the family unit. A major shift will occur in the balance of power in your relationship. The illness that made your spouse sick and helpless has put you in a dominant position. You will assume the mantle of authority in the family—along with all the responsibility—whether you want it or not. You are now in sole charge of the family finances, even if you were not before. You get to haggle about car repairs and a new roof on the house. You are now not only the provider but also the chief nurturer for your children. After a full day's work, you cook, run car pools, and pack lunches for school, and all these tasks are carried out while helping your spouse cope with the loss that he or she feels in not being able to do them anymore.

As temporary or permanent head of the household you will also need to anticipate and understand the changes that your spouse's illness will cause in each of you individually, and how they will affect your relationship. How afraid is your husband or wife of the loss of self-control and self-determination? Of pain? Of death and dying? Are you overwhelmed by your duties as a long-term caregiver? Are you starting to resent your lot in life? Your lives have changed radically because of your spouse's illness. The danger is that the illness may come between you even more than it already has and threaten to destroy your marriage. Be aware of times when you distance yourself from each other because you are both angry or afraid. As gently as possible, but as firmly as necessary, be ready to confront these feelings in your spouse and admit them in yourself. Knowing how your respective feelings affect the other person as they intersect and evolve over time will help keep your marriage intact and help you to care for your mate with more compassion and understanding.

Intervention

Having learned what you could about the medical aspects of your partner's condition and what that may mean for your future together, what can you do now to contribute to his or her recovery? If your spouse is critically ill you probably think there is little you can do. You are not a doctor, so you cannot prescribe treatment. You are not a therapist, so you cannot provide rehabilitation services. But you are married to the patient, and that makes you a key player in the whole intervention, treatment, and recovery process.

Your spouse's recovery depends on the cooperative efforts of several people: doctors, nurses, therapists, and you. You must become part of the team that makes the patient well because of your unique caregiving position. If you feel capable and the other team members support you, you may want to become team manager, assuming more responsibility for coordinating the process of restoring your partner's health. This does not mean that you take over the hospital administration and put on a white coat with M.D. on the breast pocket. It does mean that you, as the one who has the patient's interests most closely at heart, make a concerted effort to assure that your spouse is getting the best medical care possible and that everyone is aware of what is being done and why.

If you understand and agree with the course of treatment being prescribed for your husband or wife (if you don't see chapter 4) and if he or she is either apprehensive or confused about it, even after the doctor has explained it several times, you are the obvious person to calm your spouse's fears and explain what is happening. Your spouse will probably come to trust the doctor to do the right thing, but he or she will more readily trust your assurance that the care is appropriate—especially if it involves serious surgery or long and painful therapy. Also, since you are now familiar with the illness and the treatment, as well as the patient, you are in a unique position to interpret your spouse's feelings about the illness and the procedures required to cure or control it so that the medical staff can be more aware and sensitive to his or her needs and concerns. A patient's anxiety level will be quite high in the early stages of critical illness, and your husband or wife may not be able to express these feelings to the physician. You become an advocate in this case, representing the patient's point of view, helping your spouse toward recovery.

Managing your partner's illness need not be a full-time job (that comes later, at home), nor do you need to be overly obtrusive. You do not need to get in the way of the medical team's efforts to restore your husband or wife to health and vitality. But you do need to make it clear through your own actions that you *are* a member of that team and you expect good teamwork. Because you are married to the patient, you have a much greater investment in his or her medical welfare than anyone else, so you want to make sure that all team members are giving their optimal attention to your spouse's treatment and recovery. Learn to read the medical chart. You have the right to study it. It is usually located either at the foot of the patient's bed or at the nurse's station. Understand what it says about tests and medications and other medical procedures. Quite often, in cases of serious and long-term illness, the treatment plan gets extremely complicated and foul-ups can occur. They can be avoided, however, if someone has an overall picture of what is being done for and to your spouse. That someone should be *you.* If you wonder if this is not the job of the attending physician who has both skills and primary responsibility for restoring your mate's health, I must say, "Yes . . . but." Yes, your physician is skilled and responsible, but he or she is only human and on occasion could use some help. The doctor who is in charge of your spouse's case no doubt cares for several other patients and is almost always overworked. My experience and observation has been that most doctors are open to the responsible and informed questions and opinions of caregivers when they contribute to the patient's well-being. You do not need to claim expertise; I am talking about using your common sense.

Just be close to the treatment plan and be aware of the kind of care your spouse is receiving. If you see an obvious discrepancy, bring it to someone's attention—the attending physician or the primary care nurse. Make sure everyone is following "doctor's orders." Make the team that is responsible for your partner's medical care accountable to your partner and to you.

Involving yourself in the treatment of your spouse's critical or chronic illness in this way will prove fruitful for everyone—the patient, the medical staff, and especially for you. Managing your partner's care, even to the limited extent that you can in the hospital, will put you right in the middle of things, which can cause problems, but it is the best and perhaps the only place to get a true working perspective on what your spouse is going through and what you can do to relieve suffering. So get involved and intervene—your future may depend on it.

Outcome

What of the future? How will the illness turn out? Will your husband get better? Will your wife be chronically ill for the rest of her life? Is death imminent? Even as you are facing the initial stage of your spouse's illness, you cannot help but wonder about the future.

Rare is a case of critical or chronic illness in which the future is clear. Even when physicians are treating diseases with fairly predictable outcomes they are reluctant to make any long-term prognoses simply because they do not know how a particular case will end. I recall my mother asking my father's urologist how much longer he had to live in the final stages of prostate cancer, and the doctor honestly admitted he could not say. When I ask my wife's neurologist how much more improvement we can expect from the effects of her stroke, he says he just does not know.

If physicians do not know, chances are that you and your spouse will not know either. One of the biggest obstacles in critical and chronic illness is ambiguity. One of the biggest responsibilities you will have is to help your partner live with that ambiguity. There are so many things you just won't understand in the early stages of an illness or disease that it is impossible to know how it will all turn out. Is your wife's cancer curable, manageable, or terminal? What will be the permanent effect of your husband's stroke? Will they find a cure for Alzheimer's disease before it is too late to help your spouse? Fear of the unknown, especially as it relates to critical illness and disease, can be as devastating as the physical effects of the illness itself.

In order to keep the whole event of your spouse's illness in a working perspective, both of you must learn to live with its ambiguity by accepting it into your relationship. Make it part of your life together, but realize it will not stay forever. As Tillich referred to creation and chaos belonging together, he also referred to the need to keep faith in the midst of both. He suggested that we all take a leap—a "leap of faith"—that would eventually reveal meaning and purpose in our lives. So as you wonder about the meaning of your spouse's illness in your lives, and how it will end, have faith that it will end well.

4

M.D.s, R.N.s, P.T.s, and You

Much of the successful management and care of your spouse's illness depends on your individual initiative as a caregiver. Learning the facts about your partner's medical situation, getting others to respect your vested interest in her or his welfare, and accepting your claim of responsibility for her or his care requires a degree of personal enterprise that can only come from you.

Forging a positive relationship with the medical staff treating the acute phase of your spouse's illness or disease is part of the process of initiating care. We spoke in chapter 3 about your need to join the doctors, nurses, therapists, and technicians as a team member, and perhaps even become the manager, in order to smooth the path for your spouse's treatment and successful return to health. Let me make it clear, though, if you have not recognized it already, that this is not a simple task. It requires at the onset of the illness that you contact those responsible for your spouse's care and that you maintain contact with them even after the acute phase of the illness has passed.

In the course of my interviews with medical professionals and caregiving spouses, I encountered a good deal of confusion about how each perceives the way that the other carries out responsibilities for patient care. Caregivers are angry with doctors who do not seem to care enough for their spouse's medical problem or have time enough to break from hospital routine and answer questions in terms they can understand. Physicians and nurses express resentment over not being understood or appreciated for their skills and over the caregiver's failure to recognize how the often extraordinary demands of their work can place severe limits on their time and energy for individual patient care.

In this and the following chapter we will attempt to bridge this gap in communication by discovering how you can help members of the medical team care for your husband or wife and how they can help you in your own caregiving role. First we will listen to what doctors say they need from caregivers like you so they may do their job better, and then, in chapter 5, we will hear from caregivers themselves about what they want from doctors to help them in meeting their responsibilities.

What Doctors Want from You

What do doctors need from you to help them do their job? What direction will doctors take from you as a caregiving spouse? All the physicians I spoke to were eager to answer these questions. It seemed to give them the opportunity to take off their lab coats, lower their defenses, and talk freely.

Harry Stevens, a Baltimore urologist who has had extensive experience in treating patients with prostate, bladder, and other forms of cancer, was one of several doctors I interviewed who claimed a personal relationship between himself and the patient's family was vital for his successful treatment of the patient. There were two things he said he needed from caregiver and patient alike in order to build that relationship. The first was honesty:

> I've had a number of patients tell their husbands or wives one thing and then both of them tell me something else. Of course what they are doing is hiding

the symptoms from me because they are afraid that I will tell them they are another sign of the advancing disease. In the end, though, they only suffer more. I can't treat what I don't know about.

The other was accurate reporting of the symptoms that a patient experiences in an illness:

The more factual information patients (and their families) can give me, the easier my job will be to make them as well as I can as quickly as I can. An accurate account of symptoms is in the best interest of the patient. I'm willing to spend more time with a patient who sees the diagnostic and treatment process as a cooperative one because things tend to go much more smoothly between us.

Here is a doctor advocating just what the patient ordered: listening, paying heed to what the patient and caregiver have to say, and taking the time to discover the truth.

A psychiatrist from Colorado who specializes in treating head-injury patients echoes Dr. Stevens's sentiments when he talks about the active involvement of the caregiving spouse in the treatment process:

Spouses need to become a part of the team in Head Injury, so I try to help them understand as much as they can about it. I don't give the standard spiel about what happens. I listen for where they are and answer their questions and concerns no matter how trivial or naïve they sound.

For him a positive relationship between caregiver and doctor is vital for the good of the patient.

In cases of severe head injury the caregiver has so much to do. The physician needs the cooperation and understanding of the spouse to explain what's in store for them and how to care for the patient in the long term.

A retired specialist in obstetrics and gynecology from California described the importance of the doctor-caregiver relationship this way:

> My practice always involved the family—mother and father and, of course, children. If anything ever went wrong, in childbirth for instance, the family had to know about it. In really serious cases, like ovarian cancer, I always encouraged the husband to support his wife in a way that I knew I couldn't as a doctor.

What Doctors Say You Can Do

These are the comments of physicians in three different specialties of medicine, all of whom claim to want what the caregiver wants: a give-and-take relationship based on mutual integrity and respect and focused on the successful treatment and recovery of the patient. And yet, reality dictates otherwise. Based on the experiences of the majority of the medical professionals and caregivers I interviewed, this desired level of communication and trust is the exception and not the rule. The rule is something else.

See if the following scenario is familiar to you. A wife meets the doctor for the first time after her husband has been taken to the hospital with a serious heart attack. Her tension and anxiety level is at an all-time high. The doctor does not know what to say to calm her and she does not know what to ask to feel better. They are complete strangers to each other, and what does pass between them is misunderstood and soon forgotten. As time passes and her husband's condition slowly improves, the wife still feels intimidated and confused by all the hospital routine and medical technology. She becomes less inclined to ask questions and less receptive to the doctor's advice and information. Things deteriorate to a point where the wife feels she has no control over her husband's medical care and thinks no one cares very much about her either.

Abbreviated and depressing as it may be, this is a fairly accurate description of the experience of many caregivers. How can situations like this be prevented from happening? How can you manage your spouse's illness? The medical professionals I interviewed reported a number of things you can do to become a full and equal participant in your spouse's treatment and recovery.

First, you should have a basic level of trust in the medical team treating your spouse's illness or disease. It is true that doctors are busy, and sometimes there are only two nurses assigned to a hospital floor with twenty-five patients, and therapy can be a long, agonizing process. However, you should try to remain convinced that the team's sole objective is the care and cure of your husband or wife, despite appearances to the contrary. If you see evidence of a lack of care by any member of the medical staff attending your spouse, report it at once to the head nurse, attending physician, or hospital administration. Instances of mistreatment and neglect do occur, according to the medical sources I interviewed, but should never be tolerated under any circumstances. There can be severe physical and mental harm to the patient and breaches of the trust on which the relationship between the doctor, patient, and caregiver is based.

Second, you should understand the medical technology used in dealing with your spouse's illness for what it is, not a means of intimidation but a tool for diagnosis and treatment. The MRI (magnetic resonance imaging) scanner may seem to be swallowing a patient into a deep black hole (and is all the more frightening if the patient is claustrophobic), but it is one of today's most effective tools for the detection of tumors, aneurysms, defective heart valves, and the like—and it is completely painless, often omitting the need for exploratory surgery. An upper GI (gastrointestinal) series of tests is a literally distasteful experience, but it is the standard procedure for detecting stomach ulcers and other digestive disorders. X rays may have become part of "defensive" medicine today, but they have always been a vital part of the diagnostic process. Blood work is tedious and sometimes painful, and the side effects of chemotherapy can be personally devastating, but all these procedures are for the ultimate good health and welfare of the patient. Focus on the end result of these procedures—not the process itself—and help your partner do the same.

A third factor that doctors look for in building good teamwork is respect. While most physicians claimed they did not need the personal admiration of patients and their families, they do need respect, both for their professional achievements and for their personal feelings and aspirations. As one young woman surgeon put it:

> People need to realize that it requires a lot of ego drive to get through the hassle and expense of medical school, internships, and residencies on your way to becoming competent in your field. And then, once you're there, tremendous demands are put on you to cure everyone's ills and meet everyone's needs. Sometimes it is impossible to do the job right. Most of the time it's just overwhelming.

Even the most cynical of caregivers would have to admit that the job of a physician or nurse is not easy. Being on duty much of the time, on call most of the time, and caring for many people at the same time is a job with enormous pressure and responsibility. If your partner's doctors take their job seriously, as most do, showing them professional and personal respect is a legitimate part of the process of building a relationship with them so they can do their job as effectively as possible.

There is a final element in becoming a full partner in treating your spouse's critical or chronic illness. One issue on which all medical professionals agreed was the need for caregivers to be informed about their spouse's condition and what is being done to cure or control it.

Caregivers should take the initiative to learn about hospital routine, and the particular duties of staff members, and about medical procedures and therapy techniques. In chapter 3 we spoke about the caregiver's need to know and how that benefits both the spouse and the patient. This assertion is reinforced by the medical community itself. Doctors need caregivers to know as much as they can about their spouse's illness. Knowledge shared between the caregiver and the professional medical staff makes for better teamwork, and the patient will obviously benefit.

This does not mean that you must completely understand your spouse's treatment plan or that you memorize all there is to know about her or his illness or disease. It does mean that you have a fairly clear idea of its cause and how it should progress and what is being done to treat it successfully. This level of knowledge, even in lay terms, will earn you a place on the team and may even qualify you as a manager!

This observation was born out of my own experience with Jackie's illness. While she was in a coma and her life hung in the balance from day to day, I made it clear to her nurses, therapists, and doctors that I wanted to be as informed and involved as possible about the course and treatment of her condition. I often spoke with her nurses, who always explained what was going on with her at the time. I was able to have regularly scheduled meetings with her attending physician twice a week, during which he carefully explained what was happening in terms that I could understand so I could respond in terms of what I wanted to do next. On one occasion, after I had read all the books I could find in the local library about strokes, I compiled four legal-sized pages of questions to ask Jackie's doctor. We met one weekday morning in the conference room adjacent to the Intensive Care Unit where Jackie was, and he patiently and thoroughly answered every question I had listed. At the end of our meeting he told me I was ready to take my board exams in neurology!

I was able to demonstrate to Jackie's medical team that I wanted to know as much about her illness as I could and wanted to take the initiative in providing for her care. While there was a limit to what could actually be done for her, we—the children and I—got involved in her care from the beginning of her stroke. The physical therapist taught us to move her fingers and limbs to help prevent contractures. The nurses taught us to "coach" Jackie to wake up, by talking to her and stimulating her by playing music and reading from her favorite books. At the head nurse's direction, I even bought Jackie a pair of high-top sneakers to prevent foot drop!

I was able to develop a very positive relationship with the members of the medical team treating Jackie's illness because they respected my need to know. What I learned about her condition and the care I gave to her were a result of their encouragement as well as my own initiative. They needed me to know what I wanted to know myself.

The medical team realizes that the care and cure of your spouse is a joint effort and you have your particular part to play. Everyone, and especially your spouse, is depending on you to learn to play it well.

5

What Caregivers Want in Return

In addition to what medical professionals need from you to do their jobs well, it is just as important to know what you want from them to help you do yours. As a member of the team treating your spouse's critical or chronic illness, you have earned certain rights and considerations that you need to claim for yourself and then apply to your role as a caregiver.

Those whom I interviewed on this issue had a great deal to say about what they wanted from their spouse's doctors in the way of understanding and support. All of them were very direct and some were visibly hostile in expressing their feelings about their relationships with members of the medical profession. Contrary to what doctors say about needing a trusting relationship with the patient's spouse and family, a number of caregivers reported altogether different experiences. In fact, if most of the physicians were willing to take off their lab coats and talk about the need for teamwork, many of the caregivers were ready to put on their gloves and fight for it!

What do you want from your spouse's medical team in return for your cooperation? How can you lay claim to your rights as a caregiver? If you are angry, how can you overcome your feelings about your situation and use them to your best advantage in caring for your husband or wife?

Involvement

Much of the irritation that seems to be an inevitable part of dealing with medical matters and hospital personnel can be alleviated if you maintain a proactive stance in relationship to those caring for your spouse. Instead of resisting the medical team's effort to heal your husband or wife, take the initiative to tell them how they can assist you in your caregiving responsibilities. If you are feeling left out of the process, affirm your marital rights to contribute to your partner's health and well-being in a way that no one else is qualified to do.

Glenn Kirkland is a retired physicist in Bethesda, Maryland. In 1977 his wife, Grace, was tentatively diagnosed with Alzheimer's disease. Since so little was known about Alzheimer's at the time, Glenn took Grace to a research clinic at the National Institutes of Health in Bethesda for further tests, which confirmed the diagnosis. The doctors were not sure of the etiology of the disease or of the time it might take to run its course. All they could say with certainty was that it would eventually be fatal.

Unsatisfied with what he had been told up to that point, Glenn decided to take the activist approach in providing for Grace's care. He spoke with other doctors in research clinics throughout the mid-Atlantic area and learned all there was to know about Alzheimer's disease. He had Grace admitted to a special research and treatment clinic for Alzheimer's patients at the Johns Hopkins Hospital in Baltimore. He constantly observed her behavior and activities while caring for her at home and reported his findings to her doctors for their reactions and suggestions for treatment. Glenn continued to care successfully for Grace until she died early in the summer of 1990.

Glenn is one of the founders of the Maryland Chapter of ADRDA (Alzheimer's Disease and Related Disorders Association). He immediately impressed me as someone

who was able to care for his disabled wife in a very inten-
tional way by engaging her doctors in the treatment
process according to how he saw her needs. He spoke to
me of his experience.

> I wanted to make the doctors aware of my determi-
> nation to help in spite of the diagnosis. I had to perse-
> vere, learning to ask the right questions about
> medical terms and procedures. I had to learn all I
> could about what they were doing in order to know
> what I was doing myself.

Glenn knew what he was doing. Because he was Grace's
husband of many years and knew her personal history
better than anyone else, and because Grace trusted
Glenn more than anyone else, he had the edge in shaping
her long-term care. While he respected the knowledge
and opinions of the medical professionals who were caring for his wife, he made his position as a member of her
treatment team clear; he wanted the others to know
what he had learned about her condition and expected
to be taken seriously. I asked Glenn to summarize his
overall feelings on what this involves.

> Educate yourself as much as possible. Be direct and
> say what you want. Be demanding and pushy if it
> ever becomes necessary. Don't handle conflict by
> getting upset or giving up your right to an opinion.
> Handle it by being prepared; most doctors will re-
> spect you for that. If they don't, find another doctor.
> The patient should never suffer because you and the
> doctor can't agree on something.

Glenn Kirkland is a good example of someone who
used his unique qualifications as a caregiving spouse to
get what he needed from the medical establishment to
help him care for his wife. Through his constant involvement with her and her doctors he was able to maintain
a degree of control over her course of treatment that

ensured her physical welfare and spared her unnecessary emotional suffering.

The right to get involved with your spouse's care and the assurance that he or she will not suffer unnecessarily are perhaps the most important things you will want from your spouse's medical team in exchange for your trusted cooperation. You may not be as informed or as persistent as Glenn was in his caregiving duties in order to get what you want from your spouse's doctors, but it is all there for you if you push for it. Changing doctors in order to gain that assurance can be done, but it may be a bit extreme in your situation and may even cause your husband or wife the harm you are trying to avoid. As team manager, you would be, in effect, firing the team captain, which means you would then need to find a new doctor and perhaps a whole new team as well. Short of that, remember that while you could not control the onset of your spouse's illness or disease, you do have some influence over its course of treatment. No physician or medical professional will work without your or your spouse's permission, and most would prefer to work with your encouragement and support. With this provision in mind you will have more assurance that your husband or wife will be treated with all the care and competence you feel is necessary.

Influence

Gaining more influence over the team and its management of their partner's illness is something that caregivers seem to want. Wherever I brought the subject up across the country, they would invariably state their desires for more available medical staff, better channels of communication with the attending physician, and medical information given in terms they could understand. One woman I met at a support group in Maryland whose husband had a stroke three months after they were married speaks for many in her situation.

You've got to demand information. I was a docile housewife before this, and I had to grow into an independent adult real fast. I used to ask doctors about what to do next, and when they didn't know I would just say okay. Then I learned to press them for time and answers, and believe me now I get both.

She gives an example of what she learned and how it helped in caring for her husband and herself.

I once asked a doctor for advice on dressing my husband. Do you know how hard it is to put socks on someone when they've had a stroke? I hate socks! The doctor looked at me like I was a fool and then started to tell me *why* it was difficult—from a medical viewpoint, that is. I stopped him during a pause and told him I probably should ask someone in the physical therapy department. I did, and they helped me.

Caregivers do not want to be patronized or deceived, even unintentionally. They want to be treated with dignity and respect. Perhaps the doctor did not know how to put socks on a stroke victim. In cases where doctors cannot help or do not know something, caregivers want them to admit it. The wife of a head injury patient from Arizona wrote to me that "doctors don't know, and they don't know that they don't know." She may have been overstating the case, but her comment is well founded. It reflects the great frustration that many caregivers feel when they are not taken seriously by the other members of their spouse's medical team. Caregivers want the basic integrity of their relationship with the team recognized and respected.

Information

Such integrity also requires that, when doctors do know something important about an illness or disease, they feel obligated to talk about it. Many caregivers complain about the selectivity of physicians in disclosing pertinent facts about the patient's condition. Most caregivers attribute this to doctors wanting to protect them from things such as preliminary test results that spell bad news and not wanting to burden the patient or the family with what they consider unnecessary and complicated medical information. Others, however, claim that this practice has its deleterious effects. John, whose wife was suffering from an inoperable brain tumor, spoke with me during an interview in North Carolina.

> Whenever I spoke with her doctors I came away angry. They left out a lot of what I always thought they knew. I felt they only told me what they thought I needed to know in order to cope with her situation. It was only in the end that they told me everything, and at that point there wasn't much left to tell.

Even if there is not much to tell, or if the news is complicated and painful, caregivers want to decide for themselves whether or not to hear it. The doctors' reluctance to disclose certain information may be based on the best of intentions, but caregivers want the right of self-determination. Many caregivers want the whole truth when it comes to information about the care and cure of their spouse's illness or disease.

Once the diagnosis is made and the treatment plan is established, physicians can perform another valuable task. They can inform the caregiver of additional treatment and support services available beyond those offered by the hospital or clinic handling the initial care. A caregiving wife I met at a stroke activity center in California told me of her experiences with her husband's physicians.

> I wish our doctors had told me about this place from the beginning. It seemed like weeks before anyone would answer my questions about getting help with therapy. By the time we arranged things I was in a panic.

Another caregiving wife of a stroke victim had a more positive experience with her husband's physician.

> He was very helpful. I wanted to meet the social worker, and he asked her to come into his office to see me. She explained what a discharge plan was and how we could find rehabilitation services after my husband left the hospital. It was way too early to put this into effect, but at least I felt like I knew where we were headed.

As team captains, physicians are in a position to fulfill the family's need for long-term care information and support from the earliest stages of the illness. Through personal knowledge or by referring the caregiving spouse to other members of the staff, especially therapists and hospital social workers, they provide access to services available for the patient's further treatment and recovery and opportunities for the caregiver's own support. While this kind of initiative may not be a part of the attending physician's actual job description, it does go a long way in dispelling the caregiver's impression that doctors choose not to be open and cooperative in sharing the responsibility for deciding what is best for the patient's care.

As a caregiving spouse you want help from the doctors and other members of the medical team. It's that simple. You want their time and their attention, and you need to know what they know in plain straightforward terms. You want your individual dignity affirmed and your loving concern for your mate's health and welfare respected.

As a caregiving spouse you deserve all this. As the team manager of your partner's illness or disease you have the right to expect it. If you are willing to ask for it early in your relationship with the treatment team, chances are that you will receive the cooperation you want and the possibility of eventual conflict will be greatly diminished.

Sensitivity

There are two other areas of concern in which caregivers expressed what they want and need from physicians and other members of the medical team caring for their husbands or wives. The first relates to the level of emotional sensitivity that health professionals demonstrate in their relationships with patients' spouses. The other is the physician's awareness of the legal implications of his or her medical decisions. The incidents that brought these concerns to my attention were poignant enough to remind us all once again that a mutually supportive and informed relationship between the caregiving spouse and the other members of the medical team is absolutely essential to the health and welfare of the patient.

Dora is a caregiving wife whose husband, Fred, is suffering from the beginning stages of Alzheimer's disease. She is seventy-two and the sole caregiver for her husband, who is seventy-five. They live in a small town in upstate New York where it is difficult to get professional help for his condition, since the nearest clinic that specializes in the treatment of Alzheimer's patients is approximately seventy-five miles away.

Dora does get some support from friends in the community who have become aware of Fred's memory lapses and behavioral problems. However, because they are unfamiliar with the progressive deteriorating effects of Alzheimer's disease and because she is so far away from the professional support she needs to cope with her husband's illness, Dora feels increasingly isolated and angry.

She is especially angry at Fred's doctors for not showing the kind of emotional sensitivity she feels is necessary in responding to her husband's condition. One incident in particular illustrates the degree of Dora's anger and frustration in dealing with the clinic staff and her husband's situation in general.

> It was the second time we had been there after they were pretty sure that Fred had Alzheimer's. He was still hoping for the best when the doctor came in and said to me that the situation was hopeless. That's all he said, really; he wasn't encouraging about anything. When Fred heard this he just put his head in his hands and cried. I wanted to kill that doctor, and then I wanted to take Fred to a nursing home and leave him there and run away from everything.

As a caregiving spouse, Dora needs a lot of help. However, the one thing she and her husband need most, the professional understanding and support of the physician, seems to elude them. The physician obviously failed to recognize the emotional impact of his pronouncement that Fred's case was hopeless. For Fred it was a virtual death sentence. For Dora it raised to the breaking point her level of anxiety over her ability to care successfully for her husband. She could only imagine an escape from her responsibilities rather than meeting them head on— as painful as that may be.

Dora's situation illustrates the need for physicians and other health-care professionals to be ever mindful of the initial fear and the eventual sense of loss that a patient feels when faced with an illness like Alzheimer's or heart disease or cancer. And they must also realize that while every person who is diagnosed with a critical or chronic illness is afraid, virtually everyone has great initial expectations for recovery. Doctors must learn to be "patient" themselves as their patients work through the emotional

conflicts and contradictions that accompany a serious illness, and they must be caring and supportive of the patient in that process. For caregiving spouses like Dora to
do their jobs, the practice of good medical care must
include a physician's attention not only to the body but
also to the mind and soul of the patient. Such concern
makes the job of caring for a stricken husband or wife
that much easier, and caregiving spouses need and ap-
preciate it.

Awareness of Legal Consequences

Frank is a stroke victim. Before he was taken ill he and
his wife, Marge, lived in a retirement community in the
Southwest. Since his stroke Frank has lain paralyzed in
a nursing home, drifting in and out of consciousness,
being fed through a tube in his stomach. His prospects for
meaningful recovery are extremely poor. Marge visits
her husband almost daily and tries to comfort and care
for him as best she can. She wonders how all this ever
happened and is very bitter over the fact that it did. One
comment made in the course of our interview sums up
her feelings about her husband's situation very well:
"You wouldn't even want to treat a pet this way."

The fact that Frank is being force-fed in a nursing
home and Marge is powerless to do anything about it is
a result of his doctor's failing to consult with Marge when
they made a crucial decision about Frank's health care.
The doctor did not inform her about the legal consequences of their decision before they acted on it. Neither
Marge nor her husband wanted the food tube. They had
discussed its use together when Frank was still rational
and decided it would only prolong his suffering. Frank
was aware that the end was near and was preparing
himself for death, and Marge was willing to support him
in his action. The doctors recommended that the feeding
tube be inserted as his condition worsened and per-
suaded Marge to agree to it as a last-ditch effort to save

Frank's life. What they did not do, though, was tell Marge
that, once the tube was in, it could not be removed without a court order, which would be extremely difficult and
expensive to obtain. The net result of all this is, of course,
that Frank was then transferred to a long-term care facil-
ity where he is being kept alive against his and his wife's
wishes at a cost which Marge informed me is in excess of
$4,000 a month.

Marge and Frank's experience serves to illustrate only
too well that health-care professionals should be aware of
the legal consequences of their actions. Marge does not
believe that her husband's physicians intentionally deceived her into consenting to the food tube. She feels
they were using their best judgment in trying to preserve Frank's life. Her complaint is that they were appar-
ently unaware of the fact that their decision would
legally obligate Marge to a course of action prolonging
Frank's life, which neither of them ever wished to pur-
sue. Now she has no choice.

Marge's complaint is a valid one for all caregiving
spouses to consider. Perhaps the doctors did not know
what would happen once the food tube was inserted, but
they should have. They should have been sufficiently
informed of their legal responsibilities to give Marge the
option of rejecting the food tube in accordance with
Frank's expressed wishes. Health care is becoming as
legally complicated today as it is technologically advanced. Health professionals need to know how the application of their skills affects the patient's welfare—not
only according to sound medical practice but according
to the law as well. What a physician knows about medicine will undoubtedly help the patient. What a physician
doesn't know about the patient's legal rights and the
caregiver's legal responsibilities may harm both beyond
the physician's ability to heal.

When you need information that will influence a decision about your spouse's health care, you have the right
to expect full disclosure from your spouse's health care

team of everything that is pertinent to that decision. As team manager, you do not want to be left out at any point in the caregiving process. What you and all caregivers want is enough control over that process to be sure it will work to your partner's advantage.

6

Caring for Your Spouse at Home

Hospital stays precipitated by the onset of a critical illness or disease can be quite long. Your spouse has gone into the hospital and seems to be staying there forever, and you begin to wonder if things will ever change. Your visits, the hospital routine, the treatment process with all its possible complications, even your own anxiety about your spouse being there, all seem to blend together and become a given part of your life as a caregiver. But like everything else in life, good and bad, the acute phase of your spouse's illness does end and he or she becomes well enough to leave the hospital and come home.

This is a long-awaited and much anticipated event in your lives together. It is a reunion, a celebration. It is what you have worked for ever since your spouse entered the hospital. It is a return to normal. It is *home.*

In this chapter we will look at the issues involved in caring for your spouse at home. Depending on the initial severity of the illness and your spouse's present level of recovery, your duties can range from the very simple to the extremely complicated. With any serious illness that includes a return home from the hospital, there is room for a declaration of victory, a cure—even if it's only a partial one. However, as a caregiver you will need to temper your joy and enthusiasm with a dose of reality. You will need to keep things in the same perspective at home that you did in the hospital. You already know that your mate's illness had caused major changes in your relationship. Those changes will be all the more evident now that you are both under the same roof. As you wondered in the hospital if things ever would change, you must now face the question at home of whether things will ever be the same. Will life return to normal again? The answer is no—at least not for a long while and possibly not ever. You and your partner will have to accommodate change into your lives together. You will have to adjust to a different kind of normality as you continue your caregiving responsibilities and your husband or wife continues the recovery process. What then are the preliminary considerations and practical applications of home health care as you and your spouse rebuild your lives as a married couple living with the effects of critical or chronic illness?

Planning for Discharge

Caring for your husband or wife at home is a process that began before he or she ever left the hospital. If your spouse suffered a stroke or heart attack or had serious surgery, you know as well as anyone that he or she will not be fully recovered upon discharge. Leaving the hospital does not amount to a break from giving or receiving medical care; in most cases it is merely a transition to a less intensive level of care—at home, where you are the primary caregiver. Obviously you are going to need help. You need a discharge plan.

In most hospital situations discharge planning is handled by the social services department, although in larger medical centers there may be a separate office to handle this responsibility. As with other aspects of hospital routine, it is important that you understand how the discharge procedure works in order to assure that you and your spouse get the maximum advantage in providing for follow-up care at home.

First, find out who is responsible for devising a plan for

your spouse's home health care. Is it the social worker
assigned to your case, who gathers and coordinates vital
information from your spouse's medical team for successful home care? Or is it the primary-care nurse, who simply tells the hospital's "patient representative" what to
tell you about caring for your mate on your own? Find
out who is in charge. Also, find out how much your social
worker or discharge planner knows about supportive
medical services you may need for your spouse at home.
Does she or he know, for instance, where you can obtain
services that are professional and dependable, yet reasonable in cost? What about physical or occupational
therapy if your husband or wife is physically unable to be
an outpatient at the hospital or rehabilitation center?
Where do you go for medical equipment if you need it,
such as a hospital bed, a wheelchair, or a simple walker
that your spouse may need to get around? And, of vital
importance, how much will Medicare or your medical
insurance plan pay toward the costs of these services?
The chances are that the medical team that treated your
partner in the acute phase of his or her illness will not
know the answers to these questions, but your discharge
planner should—or at least should know where the answers are.

In addition to talking with the social worker in planning your spouse's follow-up care at home, you may also
want to involve other people in the process. It is per-
fectly reasonable, for instance, to request a meeting with
the attending physician to discuss the discharge plan.
Does the doctor know anything in particular that you
should know about your spouse's home health care?
What should you look for, hope or not hope for, in terms
of further recovery? Does the doctor make house calls if
that ever becomes necessary? If not, what about a referral to another specialist who does, or can future medical
matters be handled by your family physician? What
about medication? If a prescribed medicine produces
painful side effects, should you stop giving it before you

call the doctor? These and other questions need to be answered before discharge and should become part of the plan itself. Also, talk to your spouse's nurse, or the therapists if they have been involved. Find out who knows what about home health care and talk to them. In fact, talk to everyone who has been associated with your spouse's care while he or she was a patient in the hospital.

When Jackie was discharged from Montebello Rehabilitation Hospital in Baltimore, I was told by the social worker assigned to her case that I would not be having a discharge conference with her alone; instead, there would be a discharge staffing involving every member of Jackie's medical and rehabilitation team. Rather than sitting down with one person to review the comments and suggestions of everyone else regarding Jackie's care at home, I met with the entire staff itself: physiatrists, nurses, psychologists, physical, occupational, and speech therapists, the hospital dietitian, and the social worker who coordinated the meeting. It was an invaluable experience for me as each member of the team assessed Jackie's progress at the hospital and her potential for further improvement. I had the opportunity to ask pertinent questions about her care at home and learned, contrary to the previous diagnosis, that Jackie could be recovering from her illness more as a head injury survivor than a stroke victim. That meant her recovery process might well extend for six, eight, or even ten years rather than the six months to a year or more that is usual for stroke victims. The impact this news had on me at that time and the effect it had on my attitude as a caregiver have been extraordinary. I would never have been as impressed with Jackie's chances for recovery or as motivated to participate in the process if I had received this information secondhand in the course of a simple and abbreviated discharge interview!

The first phase in planning for the return of your spouse to normal must begin in the hospital if home health care is going to be even moderately successful. In a very real sense, if your husband or wife is coming home to recover from a very serious illness or to live with a chronic one, your caregiving duties are just beginning to get into high gear. Do not let the euphoria of the moment deceive you into thinking that you can do your job without help or without a plan. You will need both to be a real helpmate.

Facing Your Emotions

In addition to devising a workable discharge plan you will also want to make some emotional preparations for your spouse's return home. You will need to confront your own feelings and misgivings about living with and caring for your mate as you face up to the changes that this homecoming will bring into your lives.

How do you really feel about your husband or wife coming home from the hospital? Elated? Thankful? Relieved? Now think about what you are in for if your mate is coming home still suffering from the chronic effects of cancer, stroke, or multiple sclerosis. How do you feel about that? Frightened? Confused? Angry? Bear in mind these feelings will probably last a lot longer than the initial positive ones.

Whenever we are faced with a situation we are not sure about, like caring for an ill spouse at home, we naturally become anxious or afraid. Think about the responsibility—the health and welfare of your husband or wife is in *your* hands now. That can be a very frightening prospect to consider. Carol, a caregiver whom I met at a head injury support group in Maryland, described her feelings when she began to realize what she faced when her husband came home from the rehabilitation hospital.

> Chuck was in a motorcycle accident. There was only so much they could do for him. Now that he's coming home it's all up to me. *Why me?* I'm just so overwhelmed by this. I'm afraid I can't take care of

him. Thank God he at least has an electric wheelchair so he can get around. But if it broke down I couldn't help. I've never even changed the battery in our car, so what can I do here?

Carol has a lot of anxiety about Chuck's return home and a lot of irrational fears. She could certainly learn to change the battery in Chuck's wheelchair, but that is not the point. The point is that she is afraid to face her responsibilities as a full-time caregiving wife, afraid she cannot do the job.

Along with her fear Carol also expresses her confusion over caring for her husband. She feels overwhelmed. What *can* she do here? Confusion is often mixed with doubt and masks our feelings of ambivalence in certain situations. Carol is not only saying she is afraid she cannot do the job for Chuck, she is saying she really does not *want* to. Carol wants to rely on medical technology and personnel to do the job for her. She knows she has a major responsibility toward her husband, yet she would rather avoid the whole thing.

Carol is also angry. *"Why me?"* she asks emphatically. Quite often the question "why" is used in anger. Why did this happen to Chuck? Or, more to the point for Carol, why did it happen to her? She looks at what lies in front of her as the caregiving wife of a permanently disabled husband, and sees her whole marriage, her whole life, changing—and not for the better. Carol resents the change. She's angry over having no choice but to accept Chuck as he is, especially when she has no clear idea of how to care for him.

Is Carol a bad wife? Does she no longer care for her husband? Of course not. In ascribing these feelings to Carol I am simply pointing out some very real feelings that all of us go through in caring for our spouses at home. In mentally preparing yourself for your long-term caregiving duties, you can expect to feel afraid of what you have to do, and you will on many occasions (some more desperate than others) want to avoid your responsibilities altogether. You can also plan on getting angry at your spouse, when he or she makes mistakes or when things get out of control. Just remember, when things begin to unravel do not blame yourself. Do not feel guilty. Fear, uncertainty, and anger are natural parts of the caregiving process, and they will be all the more apparent on the home front. Learn to accept them into the process itself. They will lose a lot of their character and effect, and you will become stronger and more confident in facing your caregiving duties at home.

Setting Up a Routine

Once you have made the necessary preliminary plans for your spouse's return home from the hospital, you are faced with implementing the caregiving process itself. What was once anticipated is now a reality. Where do you go from here? What are the practical applications of caring for your husband or wife at home?

Your daily routine, which changed when your spouse became ill and went to the hospital, is about to change again now that he or she is recovering at home. Your lives will take on a new regimen revolving around the residual or chronic effects of your spouse's illness. Mealtimes, bedtime, making time for doctor and therapy appointments, and finding time for friends and family all depend on how you respond to the needs brought on by your partner's illness or disease. Does your husband require a special diet to be served at other than normal mealtimes? Does your wife's need for prolonged rest during the day interfere with establishing a regular therapy schedule? Is it difficult to attend social functions because you have so many other things to do at home? The demands that illness places on you as a caregiver may or may not be extraordinary, but they will be constant. It is important that you take control of the situation and establish a workable routine. Don, whose diabetic wife, Joanne, was told in the hospital that she would have to go on kidney dialysis, speaks about taking control of his life:

> Joanne's illness has always been a part of our lives so I wasn't surprised at the news. But now it put a major crimp in my time to care for her, and I knew I had to make some changes. I requested my schedule at work be rearranged; I told our children they would have to start taking their mother to the hospital when I couldn't, and I appealed to our close friends for more help at home.

To live with the increasing demands of his wife's debilitating illness, Don had to make some demands of his own. He needed to enlist the cooperation of his employer, his family, and his friends in providing the extra care his wife required. They became a necessary part of his daily and weekly routine.

The level of responsibility you face in caring for your spouse at home will depend on either the progressive nature of the disease or the speed of your spouse's recovery. Whatever the prospects are, your caregiving duties will fall into a routine that will take up as much space and time as you allow. The key to establishing a workable routine in home health care is not to let your caregiving responsibilities take over your life. To do that, you must be willing to make demands on others and make compromises with yourself. If you need help in routine caregiving, ask for it. Those who care about you will respond. If there is just too much for you to do on your own, decide what you can do without and let it go. Keep your sights set on establishing an orderly routine in your lives together at home. It will prove vital to your peace of mind and to your spouse's further recovery.

Setting Up a Home Health Care Team

Ever since the critical event, caring for your husband or wife has been a team effort and you have been the manager. Now that your mate has left the hospital the game plan does not change, but the players do. You will have to find and train a new health care team. Your spouse's physical condition and emotional state of mind, along with the kind of routine you have been able to establish in your lives together, will determine the kind of team support you will need in caring for your mate at home.

A good place to start building your home health care team is with your family physician, who, unless your spouse has been referred to a specialist, will more than likely take over the primary care from the attending physician in the hospital. Every winning team needs a good consultant. Make your family physician yours. Discuss the prescribed home health care plan to make sure he or she is in agreement and ask for recommendations on where the services required for your spouse can be found.

Because of the increasing insurance restrictions on medical treatment in acute care and even rehabilitation hospitals, outpatient services are becoming a whole new growth industry in our society. There are home health care agencies offering nursing care, companionship, homemaking, and respite care services. There are medical equipment companies supplying everything you could possibly need to provide for your spouse, ranging from ostomy bags to hospital beds to therapy and traction equipment. Some agencies provide physical, occupational, speech, and even recreational therapy at home and others provide these services and more on a daily outpatient basis at well equipped and fully staffed private therapy centers. There are public and private agencies offering psychological counseling services for your spouse. There are private and public transportation services available to take those who are disabled to treatment facilities.

Ask your doctor to evaluate these and other services that you may need in caring for your spouse at home. If your doctor doesn't know enough about them, look else-where for recommendations. Go back to the social worker at the hospital for an update on the services you have discovered you need, now that your husband or wife is home. Consult with friends and acquaintances who have used various home health care agencies in the past. There are even agencies to evaluate and refer home health care services for you. Use them if necessary. They usually charge a fee, but it may be well worth it.

In putting a home health care team together it is essen-tial to know who the players are, how well they perform their services, and how they will fit into your routine at home. Once you have gotten names and recommenda-tions, begin your own personal inquiry. Talk to the peo-ple who manage the agencies whose services you will be needing, and talk to the people who will actually provide them. Be a comparison shopper. Get all the information you can. Ask question, *lots* of questions.

Is the home health agency you have chosen a full ser-vice agency or is it basically a referral service that pro-vides warm bodies without recommendation or discretion? What will the home health care professionals do besides furnish basic nursing care? Will they fix meals, clean house, or stay overnight if necessary? Is the agency accredited by the state? Is it certified for Medicare? Most insurance companies will not pay for home care services unless the agency meets both of these last requirements. Does the agency carry liability insurance? Bonding is not enough; it only protects you against employee theft. You need additional financial protection in the event of pro-fessional malpractice.

When dealing with medical supply houses, make sure that the one you choose can provide everything you need in the way of equipment, services, and personal consider-ation. If you are buying equipment, ask about guarantees as you would with any other home appliance. If an item is expensive, such as a wheelchair, ask about extended terms of purchase. What about renting? Find out if it is cheaper to rent than to buy. What about service? Does the agency provide maintenance on their equipment? Will they come to your house for repairs or for the installation of safety equipment on stairs or in the bathroom? Will they show you and your spouse how to use what they rent or sell you, such as respirators, medical alert systems, and traction equipment? Finally, is your supplier certified by Medicare? Not all of them are and, as is the case with home health care agencies, insurance companies rarely do business with those who are not Medicare approved. It is to your obvious financial advantage to find this out before obtaining expensive medical equipment and supplies. In addition, almost all suppliers will bill Medicare and insurance companies directly, so you don't have to do it.

Another service your spouse may require at home is therapy—physical, occupational, or speech therapy. When choosing a therapist, either at home or at a rehabilitation center, do not assume that everyone's level of skills and dedication in working with your husband or wife will automatically be the same. Make sure you understand what kind of therapy your spouse actually needs and then look for the best person to do the job. Physical therapists provide help with regaining strength and basic mobility for walking, climbing stairs, getting in and out of automobiles, or simply learning to turn over or sit up in bed, if that is the optimum therapeutic goal. Occupational therapists will teach your spouse how to cope with the problems of everyday living. If your mate was injured on the job or in a car accident, an occupational therapist can show how to compensate for the disability in dressing, eating, getting in and out of the bathtub, or just learning to go out into the community. Speech therapists usually work with those who are suffering from the effects of brain trauma due to stroke, brain tumor, or head injury. They can help your spouse regain lost speech and memory capabilities through an individually tailored treatment plan.

When choosing therapists to join your home health team, make certain they possess the temperament and skills to treat your spouse's specific disability successfully. Pick people who you feel are compatible with your spouse's personality and will demonstrate the necessary patience. Make sure they fully explain the therapeutic goals to both of you and that you are involved in the treatment program to the extent that you can and want to be. Make sure that therapists are professionally certified. Physical therapists are licensed by the state. Occupational therapists are licensed by the American Occupational Therapy Association. Speech therapists must hold a Certificate of Clinical Competence, which is granted by the American Speech-Language-Hearing Association only after extensive graduate training and professionally supervised experience. Finally, when choosing a therapist, check to see what types of therapy are covered by your medical insurance and for how long. It is important that you have this information in hand before therapy begins, since insurance companies are rather selective about their terms of coverage. Most policies, for instance, will pay the costs of physical therapy, but many will not cover occupational therapy, even though the goals and benefits are often similar. Payment for any kind of therapy is often limited to a certain number of sessions during a fixed period of time, usually twelve months, and will cover only a percentage of reasonable charges after an up-front deductible amount has been paid. If your spouse needs therapy, know what your policy provisions are in the event that your coverage ends before the course of therapy does. Therapy is often necessary for recovery or maintenance, and without insurance coverage it is always expensive.

As your husband or wife continues to recover, other services may be required to aid in his or her return to health and to a useful life in home and community.

Perhaps, after a few weeks at home, constantly together, your partner has been in your company long enough and must literally get out of the house and away from you for a while just for a change of scenery. Perhaps, in the course of the confinement and the difficulties with the therapy or with adjusting to a new routine at home, your spouse may have become morose or depressed. On the brighter side, perhaps your husband or wife has recovered enough to want to go back to work, even if he or she cannot return to the old job. Or maybe you as a caregiver want some time for yourself, a respite from your caregiving duties. To meet these and other needs, many community services provide day care, respite care, personal adjustment and vocational counseling, job placement, and more. We will discuss these services in greater detail in chapter 7, but the home health care services we have discussed are normally available to help your mate reach his or her maximum level of recovery. The key to effective home health care is to use these services with minimum expense and difficulty to you and with maximum advantage to your husband or wife.

Motivating Your Spouse

In the midst of establishing a daily routine and building an effective home care health plan, it is possible to overlook one source of information and support that you as a caregiver may find immensely helpful: your own husband or wife.

To the extent that he or she is able, your mate should play an active role in determining the kind of care needed to facilitate recovery. In many cases these spouses have helped plan their own home health care, and some have even managed the whole process themselves. But when a spouse is suffering from a critical or chronic illness, motivating him or her in the direction of self-care and independence becomes a major task for the caregiver.

If you find yourself in this situation, how do you motivate your partner to assume more responsibility for reaching an optimum level of recovery? How can you help such persons help themselves and you in the process of being a caregiver? There are a number of things you can do.

First, try to understand how your spouse feels after suffering a serious illness, having been in the hospital, and now facing a long period of convalescence at home. Try at least to understand his or her feelings and, as one of my seminary professors used to say, try to "meet them where they are."

Of course, you cannot be exactly where these people are. You are not the victim of illness or disease; your partner is. However, as a helpmate, you may come closer than anyone else. Recognize the sense of helplessness and frustration and the loss of self-esteem. Be sensitive to your spouse's anger and sadness over having to depend on you for welfare and support. You won't be able to get into your partner's skin and feel for him or her, but you can learn what he or she feels like. We all have similar feelings at critical periods in our lives, and we can learn to recognize them in others.

If you are successful in sharing in your spouse's feelings about his or her situation, the next step is to let your spouse share in yours. A good way to motivate your partner to help with health care is to tell the truth—that you need help to get the job done. After all, one of the motives you have in caregiving is to see your husband or wife take more responsibility in getting well. You will want to maintain a level of communication with your spouse that is as direct as possible. Be honest with your mate and face facts together. The facts are that sometimes you are as afraid and angry as he or she is and you would welcome help if he or she is willing and able to give it. Letting your spouse in on the truth about your feelings and into your life as a caregiver will make the caretaking experience shorter and easier for each of you.

Admitting that you need help in an open and honest

manner should lead to the question of what your spouse can do to assist in the home health care process. Can your husband help in establishing the daily routine around the house? Can he help to clean or cook or do other household chores? Can your wife help in choosing a home health care team by doing some preliminary research on a particular agency or sitting in on interviews with nurses and therapists? Can she make critical judgments about potential therapists? If you ask for help you should expect to receive it and you should let your husband or wife do all that he or she can for himself or herself. Becoming motivated through your encouragement and support to recover lost confidence and self-esteem is the key to the ability to provide for oneself and is critical to the whole process of home health care.

Be aware, however, that the success of the home health care process may not be as easy for you to handle as it sounds. At some point you must realize that you have all the help you asked for, and you have given as much as you can, and it is time to let your spouse take increasing responsibility. You must let your husband or wife take gradual ownership of the caregiving process, which is not easy because you have done it for so long by yourself. To compensate for your own loss here, take stock in your accomplishments up to that moment. You have overcome the obstacle of motivating your spouse toward greater health and independence. You have helped him or her find new meaning in life and look forward to a future you can share together. In short, your spouse is getting well, and you have done your job as a caregiver!

7

Family, Friends, and Community Support

When your husband or wife first came home from the hospital to stay, you had some idea of what your responsibilities would be as a caregiver. Now he or she has been around the house long enough for you to know for sure.

It's work—hard work. You may be loving, dedicated, and energetic, willing to do everything you can to help your spouse get well, but even as your caregiving efforts begin to pay off with evidence of his or her increased health and independence you find the basic tasks of home care more tedious and exhausting for you and less appreciated by and helpful to your spouse. You begin to realize that you cannot continue to do your job without finding some additional assistance for both of you.

At this point in the home health care routine you look for some relief from your work load as a caregiver and seek additional help for your spouse's recovery. Not only can you call upon professional agencies and therapists, but you can also create a network of extended support for each of you composed of family, friends, and additional specialized services in the community. The management of your spouse's illness has always been a cooperative effort, and now, as other needs besides therapy and nursing begin to arise, your home health care team will grow to accommodate your changing situation.

In this chapter we will learn how this supportive network can be established. We will see how to enlist family and friends as sources of support in the process of helping your husband or wife. What real use can family and friends be at a time like this? What needs to be done for you that will also help your mate and how do you decide who should do what? Also in this chapter we will look at some other professional services in the community that are specifically directed to meet needs that may have arisen in the course of your spouse's recovery, including respite and day care, educational and cognitive retraining, and the various services available through vocational rehabilitation.

The Supportive Network

In my interviews and conversations across the country an overwhelming number of caregivers said they depended on family members and close friends for help in caring for their husbands or wives. This is not surprising. Spouses who realize they can no longer carry the burden of care alone will naturally turn to those they are closest to and trust for assistance. Claire, the wife of a multiple sclerosis victim, relates her experience:

> When Lou's condition deteriorated to the point where he could no longer bathe or dress himself I knew I needed more help than I was getting or could afford to pay for. So I sat down with our oldest two children and then went to Lou's parents and told them all how it was and what I needed.

Adele, whose husband has Parkinson's disease, describes her situation:

> When we moved to the beach after Charlie's retirement I knew we couldn't look to the children for help if we needed it. Now that we do need it I am glad to know we have friends in our community that I can count on to help both of us.

Family and friends are known for coming through in times of crisis. Realizing you need them and knowing they are there is both commendable and comforting. But it is just the beginning. The real issue is how to utilize the available help to you and your spouse's best advantage. How can you use the help that family members and friends are willing to give?

The first thing you need to do is to learn how to ask. That's not as silly as it may sound. Indeed, if you do not know how to appeal effectively for help, you certainly lessen your chances of receiving it. Let it be known that you need it. You might be surprised at how many in your circle of family and friends think you are "super husband" or "super wife," that you can handle it all on your own because you have never asked for assistance. Here is an instance where what they don't know can hurt *you.* Following Claire's example, sit down with those you feel you can rely on *before* you lose control of your situation and admit you need help. And then *ask* for it. Be sensible in your approach. Cry if you want, get angry if you must—but not at them. Don't demand or plead for help from people; you will either receive it grudgingly or not at all. If you honestly feel that certain family members have an obligation to help you (as Don did with his children in chapter 6), present that obligation to them in a direct and nonthreatening manner. Do not try to inspire a sense of guilt or undue responsibility in people; you will eventually be repaid with resentment and lack of attention to your spouse's needs. When asking for help, tell selected family members and friends that you care for them and trust them and that you *need* their help during this very trying time in your life. When people who love you know they are loved and trusted, they will respond in kind and do whatever they can—and often whatever you ask—to help.

Getting the right help from your family also depends on understanding your family dynamics—how well the family "works" together—under normal circumstances and under periods of stress. It is generally true that family members who are open and trusting with one another in good times will come together in mutual comfort and support in times of trouble. The same is true in reverse. Members of families whose relationships with one another are marginal at best will usually experience noticeable deterioration in those relationships when a crisis occurs.

You need to make an objective decision about where your family fits in the care continuum. It is generally true that most families do come together in times of crisis. It is equally true that most of them do not always get along with one another. The crux of the matter in getting the kind of help you need to care for your husband or wife is to anticipate how well your family will be able to respond. If your children have stood by you both throughout the length of the illness, wanting to do what they could, you have no problem. If you know what they can do for you, now is the time to ask. If you sense little else besides an obligation in your siblings or in-laws to assist you, expect little help other than what people give when they feel obligated to do so. If, however, you feel abandoned by everyone in your family at this point in the caregiving process, expect no help at all. Some families, because of unresolved feelings of guilt, anger, or fear, can be so paralyzed by the critical illness of one of its members that they are powerless to do anything that could be termed positive. If you feel this is true in your case, don't devote needless time and energy in trying to sort out these emotions. Now is not the time for family therapy. Look for help elsewhere. In any case, when looking for help from your family, look first at your family history in good times and bad so you will know what to expect and what to do.

Getting the right kind of help from your friends in caring for your spouse is also a vital part of the caregiving process. When asking friends for help you may have the advantage of a wider selection of potential caregivers, but the disadvantage is not knowing exactly what their skills and interests are.

Once you have chosen those whom you wish to assist you in your spouse's continued care, however, and they have agreed to help, you will want to match their abilities with the things that need to be done for your spouse at home. Friends who want to help are obviously well intentioned but probably not sufficiently informed as to what they can do. Make an assessment of your situation by determining what your spouse's needs are at the present time and than ask your friends what they would *like* to do to help. Create a "division of labor" by ranking your friends' skills and preferences and applying them to your needs, making sure that all needs are met in the process. This approach also works with families, and while it may sound a bit calculating, bear in mind this is one time in your life when you should use to the full advantage everyone who wants to help. When deciding who should do what, your mutual convenience and welfare should be your primary concern.

If your husband or wife needs basic companionship other than you, find a friend with patience, insight, imagination, and a valid driver's license. As you know by now, one of the things that can wear you down is being with your mate for extended periods of time, especially if she or he is dependent on you. If you are going to ask someone to fill in for you here, make sure they have the temperament to do it on a regular and long-term basis, the wisdom to accept and understand your spouse's physical or mental limitations, and the ability not just to entertain but also to stimulate your partner toward the optimal level of recovery. It will also be of great help if your friend can take your husband or wife out of the house on occasion. An afternoon drive or a visit to a restaurant, movie, or museum can be of great therapeutic value, not only to your spouse but to you as the primary caregiver.

When looking for someone to provide practical nursing care, pick a friend or family member who has had some experience in caring for the ill and is not easily embarrassed by normal or abnormal bodily functions or

intimidated by special treatment or medication procedures. Choose someone with your spouse's approval;
someone with whom your husband or wife will feel comfortable and secure in submitting to the often intimate
procedures of personal nursing care. It would be most
convenient if the person you chose was already a trusted
friend who also possessed nursing experience. If that
combination does not exist in anyone you know, pick
someone with basic nursing skills and allow for the personal relationship to grow over time.

If you need help at home with housekeeping duties
such as cooking and cleaning or running errands, you
may have a wider variety of friends from which to
choose, since these activities do not require interper-
sonal skills or prior training. You will obviously want
someone who appreciates a clean and orderly house, but
do not be too finicky if this person fails to measure up to
your own standards. You might have to make some compromises here and live with dust in the corner or under
the bed for a while. If you need personal assistance in
your cooking duties, pick someone whose culinary tastes
are similar to yours. With all the other changes in your
life, you do not need to adjust to a new diet as well. Be
sure, though, that whatever diet you follow is a healthy
one; your spouse's nutrition is a vital contributing factor
to successful recovery. Avoid fat-laden and unhealthy
foods. Your recipe for chocolate mousse or your friend's
recipe for her grandmother's fried chicken will no longer
do as part of your spouse's steady diet at home.

The old adage that "good help is hard to find" is probably as true today as it was in the past. In matching the
abilities of your friends and family to meet your partner's
needs, you must rely on the same skills in yourself that
you are looking for in others: patience, wisdom, and flex-
ibility. Occasionally, however, you will encounter the
great exception to the rule, someone who has all the
necessary skills and compassion to be your surrogate
caregiver—someone who can do it all. You may find this

person in your family or in your circle of friends at work or in your church or community. We have someone in our church who fits this category. Naomi Palmer is one who shows the true character and qualities of what it is to care for those in need. Naomi had cared for several members of her own family and her congregation and was of immense help to Jackie and me during her illness and recovery. Nothing is too much for Naomi, from housekeeping to driving friends to and from medical appointments, and with her professional nursing background she has all the necessary talents to care for her "patients" at home. As hard as you may find it to believe right now, people like Naomi do exist, and many of us have the potential to be like her when the need arises. If you are fortunate enough to find someone like Naomi just when you need him or her, accept his or her offer to help. Count it as one of the blessings that come into your life as you help your husband or wife with the struggle to overcome the losses suffered in the course of illness or disease.

One additional factor to consider when seeking suitable help from family and friends in caring for your spouse at home is a financial one. Obviously you are going to pay the professionals—the nurses and the therapists—to care for your spouse, but think about paying your volunteer staff as well. It does help. While close friends and family may be willing to assist you in any way they can, a tribute on your part shows that you care about them as much as they care about you. Money can be a touchy subject among friends and family, especially in these circumstances, but if you are as honest and sincere in offering to pay them something for their help as you were in asking for help to begin with, they should feel comfortable enough to tell you whether or not they wish to accept.

Cultivating the support of family members and friends is a vital part of your spouse's home health care. As time passes, however, and your husband or wife continues to progress toward normalcy (even if it's a new and permanently different kind), services other than what your family and friends can give to your spouse's care may become necessary. Part of your extended network of support then will include activities and programs in the community that will enhance your partner's further recovery and provide each of you with lasting benefits.

Respite Care

As we have already recognized, there will be times when you and your husband or wife have simply been at home together too long. Even having friends coming in to help is not enough to break the routine of home care. You're both suffering from cabin fever; you are on each other's nerves and in each other's way. You need rest and relaxation, preferably away from each other. For you, R and R can come in the form of respite care; for your spouse it can come through involvement in organized and supervised group activities in the community.

Respite care is exactly what it sounds like. You get time off from caring for your spouse. Family and friends may be able to help you here, but probably not on an extended or regular basis. There will be times when you simply need to get away from your caregiving responsibilities for more than a few hours. Perhaps you would like to take the day off, or even a weekend, and you don't wish to rely on friends for help, fearing it would inconvenience them. What can you do? Respite care is a possible solution. It is not a return to nursing care, nor is it exactly like family companionship. It is a professional service in which specially trained, compassionate, and responsible individuals come into your home and look after your spouse's needs for a specified period of time. Florence, whose husband lives at home suffering from Alzheimer's disease, described her experience with respite care.

Once a week a man comes to my door, but it's not to call on me. He comes to see my husband while I go out for the day to see my friends, shop, or do whatever I want. I don't feel guilty leaving Ed at home or feel like I'm saddling him with friends. I feel free for a change, and that's wonderful!

Respite care services are available through home health care and other social service agencies in the community. Sometimes they are available through other organizations, such as churches or community service clubs. Respite caregivers should be bonded, and you should check their references and those of the agency that employs them. The costs are usually an out-of-pocket expense because respite care is rarely covered by insurance or Medicare. Consider the value of the service in your own situation, however, and you may see the expense as a good investment nonetheless.

Community and group activities provide a chance for your spouse to get out of the house for a while. They can be like mini-vacations, allowing your mate to "escape" the regimen that has been set up at home and enjoy the opportunity to socialize and meet new people, many of whom may have similar deficits. It is a chance for your mate to feel good about being part of a group again and also to learn how and where he or she can fit as a productive member of the community while approaching the maximum level of recovery from illness or disease.

A number of community services meet these needs. Adult day-care centers are one of them. Adult day care has taken a bad rap over the years because it is often compared to children being closely watched in a highly supervised atmosphere. That may be necessary for children, but it is hardly something to which you as a caregiver would want to subject your husband or wife.

While there are circumstances where this level of attention is necessary, such as caring for dementia victims, adult care is much less constrained and more flexible in meeting the needs of its participants. Individual and group activities are varied and include such things as

reading, crafts, woodworking, cooking, bridge, music appreciation classes, group exercises, support groups, and
day trips to theaters, museums, and restaurants. People
are encouraged to participate in whatever they wish and
to develop interests at their own pace. They need not
conform to a rigid set of rules or expectations; rather,
they are to enjoy themselves and recapture some of the
self-esteem that their illness has taken away.

Day-care centers—or adult activity centers, as they
may be called—are sponsored by public social service
agencies, volunteer organizations, and private enter-
prises. They are located in community centers operated
by local government, in churches, in private rehabilitation centers, and in other places accessible to those who
are limited by their disabilities. Unlike most other forms
of community service, adult day care is usually quite
inexpensive and sometimes free of charge if the staff is
volunteer or publicly supported. At any rate, if your
spouse can profit from the socializing experience of adult
day care, it is a program worth considering.

Vocational Rehabilitation

Other programs that are worth your time and effort to
investigate are those that will reeducate and train your
spouse to reach his or her optimum level of participation
in the life of the community again. Once your husband
or wife has recovered to the point of being able to meet
basic needs for self-care, including bathing, dressing,
feeding, and generally looking after oneself, he or she
may want to go on to achieve an even greater level of
independence. Your mate may want to retrieve some
lost communication skills, or improve his or her educational abilities, or even go back to work.

The most accessible and widely known programs to
help your spouse achieve these goals operate in most
states under the heading of Vocational Rehabilitation.
"Voc-Rehab" is a comprehensive rehabilitation and job

training program usually sponsored by federal funds and administered by state agencies such as the Department of Education, Social Services, or Health and Mental Hygiene. It is open to all disabled state residents who wish to work but whose illness, chronic disease, or injury keeps them from returning to their previous job. Its goal is to retrain disabled persons in new vocations, enabling them to reenter the work force and achieve as much economic independence as possible.

The program works like this. Your husband is well enough to go back to work, but his physical limitations prevent him from pursuing his old career. You have contacted your state vocational rehabilitation agency, which has referred you to a local office in your area. You make an appointment for your first meeting with the counselor assigned to your case, who tells you about the various levels of service the agency offers. They begin with a complete physical, psychological, and vocational evaluation of your husband's interests and abilities in finding a new career. After your husband's vocational aptitudes and capabilities have been identified, an educational and training program will be designed to meet his stated vocational goals. That program may involve additional education in a trade school, college, or even at the graduate level. It may include on-the-job training and apprenticeship. It may involve getting your husband back into the business world or even going into business on his own. The program, whether it takes weeks, months, or even years to complete, is directed toward making your husband an economically independent and responsible member of the community again. He should even receive an initial job opportunity appropriate to his newly acquired skills and training.

The program is a comprehensive one and includes additional services to support your husband in reaching his vocational objectives. Personal adjustment counseling is available if needed. Transportation to and from counseling or medical appointments and training programs may also be part of the benefits package. If your husband needs additional medical attention such as special treatment or medication and cannot pay for it, if he needs eyeglasses or a hearing aid or even further surgery to help him go back to work, your vocational rehabilitation counselor can arrange for these services through Medicare, Medicaid, or other special funding. If your husband is eligible, your counselor can also help him apply for the appropriate disability benefits from Social Security, Worker's Compensation, or your insurance company. If he is ineligible, in some cases a living allowance may be provided.

The best feature of vocational rehabilitation, at this writing, is that all the services I have mentioned are free. A prospective client does have to qualify by passing the initial evaluation, but the costs for the program are covered by state and local funds. While public money for job training and related programs has been curtailed in recent years, vocational rehabilitation has maintained a good track record in successfully returning people to the work force. It is a service that should be available to you and your husband or wife if you wish to use it.

There are other less comprehensive but equally effective programs in the community to assist your spouse in achieving his or her highest level of independence and recovery. These programs are generally more specialized in their services than vocational rehabilitation, and often "voc-rehab" clients are referred to them if they have a specific problem or set of problems to be resolved before returning to work. Most of these are day programs and are hospital based. They treat a specific disability, providing a consistently high level of rehabilitation and care to help an individual cope with and overcome the deficits that his or her illness or disease has caused.

One such program which is representative of others around the country is the RETURN program at Sinai Hospital in Baltimore. It is a rehabilitation program for adults who have suffered brain trauma as a result of head injury, stroke, or brain tumor. The purpose of RETURN is to do just what the word says—return brain-injured persons to their maximum level of functional and economic independence in their community. As a hospital-based program it has access to all necessary medical and therapeutic services required to help its clients become more healthy and self-sufficient, including standard medical and neuropsychological care, a comprehensive therapy program, and services in special education and vocational assessment.

A large portion of the program is structured in a classroom setting in which clients are taught to improve their cognitive abilities in the areas of memory concentration, judgment, and problem solving. Class activity focuses on improving personal adjustment and communication skills and generally enhancing the client's ability to cope with the pressures and demands of everyday life.

Services are also provided on an individual and family basis. Speech and physical therapy and psychotherapy are offered to the client one-on-one. Families are invited to help in developing the client's treatment and rehabilitation plan and to learn some of the cognitive training techniques to use at home. They are also encouraged to participate in support group activities that are coordinated by the professional program staff.

The RETURN program is indicative of the kind of attention that is being given today to new approaches in rehabilitative health care. It is one of several emerging programs around the country that concentrate their caregiving efforts on solving the physical, emotional, and practical problems caused by a particular illness, injury, or disease. I can confirm through my wife's success in RETURN that the format is successful. If you believe your spouse would benefit from a rehabilitation program that specializes in treating the effects of stroke, heart attack, mental illness, or physical injury, you need to investigate the possibilities in your area. A good place to begin would be your physician, your vocational rehabilitation counselor, or the social work department at your local hospital. You may, if you have not considered it already, want to include a program like RETURN as part of your original home health care plan.

Caring for your spouse at home, watching his or her progress from a position of weakness and dependence to a position of strength and independence, is an inspiring, rewarding, and demanding experience. As you have no doubt found out in your own experience, it is something you should not and really cannot do alone. You need help along the way, and you have every right to ask for and receive it. You do honestly look forward to the day when your husband or wife is completely independent again, when he or she is as physically, mentally, and spiritually fit as possible and you have nothing more to do! In the meantime, though, you want to do all you can to contribute to the healing process. Just remember that both the extended care and support of family members and friends and professional expertise and services are available right in your community if you take the time and make the effort to find them.

8

Self-Help/Self-Care

Until now we have centered our attention on the support you have given your spouse during an illness. As a caregiver you want to do all you can to help, but at some point in the process the focus of your attention needs to shift away from your mate's health and well-being to your own.

One of the reasons I wrote this book was that you, the victim's spouse, are often the forgotten partner in the whole drama of critical and chronic illness. Your husband had a sudden heart attack. He was rushed to the hospital and placed in intensive care, where his life hung in the balance for several days. Or your wife had major surgery for ovarian cancer and has undergone weeks of chemotherapy, complete with all the side effects. Now, with your help, your spouse's health is improving. As you review all that he or she has been through with doctors and nurses, machines and medication, and pain and suffering, you realize that you have been through it too—not in the same way, of course, but you have suffered your own personal consequences.

You may have been a forgotten partner in the course of this critical illness or disease, but you do not need to remain a silent one. As your spouse emerges from the need for constant care and you from the tasks of constant caring, you have the right to ask for and expect care for yourself.

In the next two chapters we will look at some of the things you can do to have those expectations met. We will examine the need for self-care and the means by which you can find the necessary support to have a life of your own. In this chapter, we will discuss the importance of maintaining a healthy "self-preserving" attitude in the caregiving process, and we will look at the merits of joining a peer group as a source of support. In chapter 9 we will consider the issues involved in determining whether you should seek professional help in coping with the effects of your spouse's illness or disease.

The Importance of Attitude

There's no doubt about it, your partner's illness can get you down. It is also true that only you can get yourself up again. It's all a matter of having the right attitude, which, as you know by now, is not easy with all the unknowns that are part of critical and chronic illness.

Caregivers who told me what they do to handle the emotional burden of spousal support made a number of suggestions. The first was to think and be positive about your overall situation. While this may seem obvious to the point of being trite there is practical value in maintaining a positive attitude.

Elaine, a caregiver from Minnesota, talked about the importance of attitude in her situation with her husband, Tom:

> I knew from the damage Tom's stroke caused that it was going to control us if we didn't control it first. So we decided to take charge of our lives and face our loss together. We've made some compromises and given some things up. . . . I never would have believed it at first, but we are closer now than we were before Tom got sick.

It is hard to see good coming out of something as bad as a life-threatening illness, but it can happen. What is important is a positive attitude. Look for what can be learned or taken from the experience to improve your life, rather than what can ruin it, or even end it. It can be a matter of appreciation, of being thankful for the new insight, patience, and strength that were given to you in the course of your spouse's illness. One caregiver spoke of "an attitude of gratitude"; not that things could have been worse, but that she and her husband found the ability within themselves to make things better—even when her husband could not be fully healed.

Having the right attitude about your overall situation leads not only to getting the upper hand in your partner's illness but also to taking charge in important areas of your own life. For instance, if you have a job apart from your caregiving responsibilities, do all you can to keep it. Aside from the fact that you probably need the money, your job will give some continuity to your life and keep you connected with the "real" world. Even if you have to work part time or take a cut in pay and responsibility, it is important to maintain your occupational identity outside the home.

Also, maintain your circle of friends, from work or elsewhere, friends whom you have chosen not for your mate's home health team but just for yourself. If having your own friends has always been an important part of your life, it will be all the more important to you now. You will need your friends around you—to listen to and care for you quite apart from caring for your husband or wife. Your friends will help keep your own life in a workable perspective. They will help to keep you in control.

A positive attitude will also help to keep you fit. It is obvious in caring for your spouse that you need to remain healthy yourself. Your physical and mental well-being is the key to the whole process. Physical fitness depends on proper rest, nutrition, and exercise. When you go out with your friends, do not make a habit of staying out too late or indulging in a diet of restaurant and fast food. If you drink, keep your intake of alcohol at a moderate level, whether home or away. Do not become a couch potato; rather, make the effort to exercise at least four times a week for fifteen to twenty minutes a session. If that is not feasible, at least *walk* as much and as vigorously as possible. Cardiovascular experts say that walking is the best form of exercise for all of us. A good overall rule for your physical fitness is this: Follow whatever is prescribed for your spouse in the way of diet and exercise and rest for yourself and you will not go wrong.

Staying mentally fit is also important. Keeping your sense of humor is one way to maintain your mental balance, as is spending time alone. Consider making a "personal retreat" where you step away from your caregiving responsibilities, and everything else you are involved in, be it work or play, in order to focus purely on yourself for a while. Your retreat may involve slipping off for a few hours, a whole day, or even longer. It may be organized or spontaneous. Keep in mind, however, that it is to be a solitary experience, not a social one. It can be a spiritual one as well. Meditation and prayer are certainly appropriate responses to your search for new meaning and purpose in your life. Take a walk in the park, around a lake or a city reservoir. Go to the mountains or the beach in the off-season. Reflect on your life as it is now: your marriage, your work, your friends and loved ones. Think about the changes brought on by your spouse's illness and what you have learned from it and how it has affected your values and goals in life. When my wife was so desperately ill that we thought we would lose her, I made it a point to take a vigorous walk every afternoon (made all the more vigorous when accompanied by Charlie, our family dog), on which I tried to thrash out my thoughts and feelings about Jackie's expected death and my impending single life and parenthood. I found no lasting resolution to my problem during those times, but on most days I was able to affirm my belief that the necessary guidance and direction for my future would come. Even when I could make no sense of my life, my daily journey through the neighborhood was vital to my psychological health and mental stability. It helped to ensure that I maintained an attitude toward my situation that was positive and right for me. Your mental health may depend just on keeping your life in balance following your husband's slight heart attack, or it may require that you put your whole life back together after your wife has endured a shattering illness. Only time will tell what you need, but it must be quality time, alone and away.

Joining a Support Group

Support groups are relative newcomers to the whole idea of spousal support. They provide an opportunity to join with other caregiving spouses to talk about what it is like to *be* one. A painful side effect of caring for a sick husband or wife on a long-term basis is the feeling that no one could possibly imagine what it's like; you are alone. In a support group you meet people who know what it is like and you are *not* alone.

In my interviews with caregiving spouses I found increasing acceptance of the idea of peer group support. I have attended many different groups across the country and have belonged to two of them in my own community. With the right kind of leadership and compatibility, support groups work very well to help often beleaguered husbands and wives cope with the demands of caring for their sick and injured spouses at home. If you are contemplating joining a group, or thinking of sampling one because it might help, there are a number of issues to consider in choosing a group that is right for you.

First, decide what kind of group you are seeking and what you want and need from a group experience. Different types of groups offer different things to different people. Some groups meet informally on a semiregular basis just so the participants can share the emotional burden that they all carry in caring for their spouse at home. There is no set agenda or expectations other than the hope of finding kindred spirits and mutual support. Anna, whom I met on her first visit to a stroke support group in California, described what she wanted in coming to the group that day.

> I wasn't sure I should have even come. I can't really leave my husband alone; he gets very angry when I do. But I just can't stand being with him all day. We don't know anyone here. He had his stroke just after we moved down from Los Angeles. I heard about this group in the newsletter, and I thought I'd come just to talk some.

As I recall, Anna went on to talk a lot. She was lonely, miserable, and afraid. Even though she got up to leave a few times because she thought her husband would miss her, the group urged her to stay and helped her realize that her husband's petulance was really a way to manipulate and control her and that she had a right to her own life like everyone else. The group worked well that day to provide Anna with the support to take care of some of her own emotional needs.

Other groups are more formal in their structure and intent. Aside from lending support, these groups will meet, usually in a seminar or workshop setting, to dispense new and useful information on how to meet your spouse's caregiving needs. Topics of discussion can range from learning about changes in Medicare and Social Security rules to proposed legislation for the rights of the disabled, new techniques in home care for ostomy patients, and so on. These groups usually have leaders and specific agendas and meeting times. Group members usually listen and absorb knowledge rather than talk and share feelings. These groups are not meant to be an alternative to support groups but a helpful addition.

Another type of group experience is found in the formal therapy group. Therapy groups are highly structured and are run by qualified leaders with extensive backgrounds in individual and group counseling. Group members work together under the leader's supervision to resolve personal issues and improve their marriages or other significant relationships. If your caregiving duties have raised feelings that are affecting not only your life but also how you are caring for your spouse, if you are facing relationship issues with your spouse and need not only support but some fairly clear direction on what to do, it is entirely appropriate to consider group therapy as a viable source of help.

Once you have been able to decide the kind of group experience you need, the next issue is where to find it. Fortunately, there are several places to start looking, and one source usually leads to another. The best way to begin is to talk with your family physician or with the social worker at your local hospital. Family doctors are often in contact with support groups that deal with their patients' illnesses, and hospital social workers often run groups for patients and families even after discharge. Support groups are also operated by national organizations that are identified with a particular illness or disease, such as the National Stroke Association, the American Heart Association, and ADRDA (Alzheimer's Disease and Related Disorders Association). You can call their local chapters for details on meeting places and times. Service groups and organizations, such as the Easter Seal Society and the Lions Club, may operate support groups. So may churches, schools, and retirement and life-care communities. Other support groups function as a part of a network. In southern California, for example, there is an organization called the United Stroke Foundation, which operates a series of support groups throughout the greater Los Angeles area from Anaheim to Beverly Hills. The foundation helps groups to keep in contact with one another, providing support to all group members even if they move from one part of the area to another.

If you cannot find a support group or if you do not like what is available, you can always begin a group on your

own. Start looking for members in the same places you
would look to find an existing group—hospitals, church
organizations, retirement communities, rehabilitation
centers, and so forth. A group I met with in a retirement
community in North Carolina was begun by two women
who found that, while their community seemed to have
every other conceivable type of educational and entertainment activity for its residents, it had no support
groups for families and victims of critical illness and disease. Neither woman had any expertise in starting a
group other than that they were caregiving wives and
needed to share their experiences and feelings. They
placed a notice in the community newsletter, and over
a dozen caregiving spouses came to the first meeting.
The group has been growing ever since, and other support groups have started in the community as a result of
its success.

I was a member of a support group in a hospital in
Baltimore where my wife had been a patient. I joined for
two reasons: to gather material for this book and simply
to give and receive support. My experience was largely
successful on both counts, but it leads me to make a few
additional observations.

Support groups do work to provide care for caregiving
spouses. They focus on *your* feelings for a change, and
you have the opportunity to discover that you are not the
only person in the world with your particular set of problems. We are all overworked and exhausted and sometimes we are lonely and depressed and we all deserve
one another's time and attention.

When the process begins to unfold and people express
their feelings more openly, support groups become great
places to understand how to cope with all the critical
events of our life. We hear other people's stories of patience, hope, humor, tenacity, and righteous anger and
apply the benefits of their experience to our own. In my
case I learned more than I expected about spousal support and how to handle other parts of my life as well. As

I listened to people talk about how they managed to meet the physical and emotional needs of their spouses, raise children, run the household virtually on their own, pay the bills more or less on time, keep their job if they had one, and have something resembling a life of their own, I knew their story was my story and what they did to carry the day I could do also.

Support groups grant us the privilege of sharing the experience of other people with similar problems. Groups take on a life of their own from which everyone can benefit; however, like all living things, support groups can self-destruct if they are not properly cared for. The group I belonged to suffered such a fate. While it worked very well at the outset and many of us found what we were looking for, the group changed over time and eventually disintegrated. Groups may start with the best of everything—the best intentions, dedication, and potential—but they may end because there is too much of one thing and not enough of something else. In our group there were too many people over thirty, too much to be said, and not enough time for everyone to say it. Those who did not speak were tired of listening to those who did (including the few who tried to monopolize the conversation), and after a while people began to drop out. There was a last-ditch attempt on the part of the leadership to change the format from giving support to dispersing information, but that was unsuccessful.

Starting a group and keeping it together over a period of time is no easy task, whatever its purpose or attraction may be for its participants. To remain alive and well, a group must have at least three things going for it. First, groups must have a high level of leadership. The leaders do not have to be trained professionals in every instance, but they should be perceptive and understanding. They should encourage people to talk; they should be good listeners and be able to guide the group discussion in a positive and supportive direction. Second, a group needs cohesion. The members should meet together in an at-

mosphere of mutual trust and respect; they must feel
united if the process is to work. If the group is too large
or too small to be cohesive—if it cannot achieve the level
of equality and acceptance that it needs among its members—the group will literally come unglued and eventually disintegrate. And, third, a group must do what it says
it will do. It must live up to its stated intentions. A group
has to have a clearly defined goal acceptable to all its
members. Even if it is as simple as giving everyone a
chance to speak, that goal must be achieved if the group
is to be successful and the people are to be helped. Look
for these things when you are looking for a group to join,
and your chances of getting the help you want should be
better than if you join one indiscriminately.

Group support and personal introspection are two
very important and helpful means to provide care for
yourself during and after you have provided care to your
sick or injured spouse. Maintaining a positive attitude
about your life, having a realistic awareness of your wants
and needs as a caregiver, and knowing that there are
places to go to have some of them met are all necessary
to the process of self-care. Be prepared to do what is
necessary. You have assumed the responsibility of caring
for another person in your life, and you have earned the
right to demand care for yourself.

In recent years, organizations like the American Association of Retired Person (AARP) and the National Well
Spouse Foundation have published a "Caregiver's Bill of
Rights," which defines our needs and limits as caregivers
for marriage partners and other family members. I am
including the AARP version here, reprinted from *Helping An Aged Loved One* by Jo Horne, for your information and inspiration. As you can see the list is not
complete, and you are encouraged to add to it and read
over your own bill of rights on a daily basis.

A CAREGIVER'S BILL OF RIGHTS

I have the right
—to take care of myself. This is not an act of selfishness. It will give me the capability of taking better care of my relative.
—to seek help from others even though my relative may object. I recognize the limits of my own endurance and strength.
—to maintain facets of my own life that do not include the person I care for, just as I would if he or she were healthy. I know that I do everything that I reasonably can for this person, and I have the right to do some things just for myself.
—to get angry, be depressed, and express other difficult feelings occasionally.
—to reject any attempt by my relative (either conscious or unconscious) to manipulate me through guilt, anger, or depression.
—to receive consideration, affection, forgiveness, and acceptance for what I do from my loved one for as long as I offer these qualities in return.
—to take pride in what I am accomplishing and to applaud the courage it has sometimes taken to meet the needs of my relative.
—to protect my individuality and my right to make a life for myself that will sustain me in the time when my relative no longer needs my full-time help.
—to expect and demand that as new strides are made in finding resources to aid physically and mentally impaired persons in our country, similar strides will be made toward aiding and supporting caregivers.

By whatever standard you wish to apply to your situation, you will need help in caring for your spouse in times of critical and chronic illness. Even if you have not been accorded all the rights you may deserve in your caregiving duties, you still should "get as good as you give." You have the fundamental right to expect spousal support for yourself even as you continue to give it. So remember, do not be a silent partner. Help yourself by *taking* care as well as giving it.

9

Seeking Professional Help

In the process of looking for the things you need from others and within yourself to enhance your life as a caregiver, you may have acquired the right attitude, joined the right group, and gotten all the support and insight you can handle. Yet you may realize you need more than this to cope successfully with the long-term effects of your spouse's illness. You realize that you need individual professional counseling.

Many people in our society find the idea of getting professional help unacceptable. The phrase itself (along with "going to the shrink") may be taken to indicate personal weakness or failure. The prevailing opinion is that if you cannot do your duty and live up to your responsibilities on your own without help, you should feel guilty and ashamed.

Nothing is further from the truth. If you are considering counseling for yourself, you have realized that at this point you have done all you can do on your own and it is just not working anymore. You know you need help—the undivided professional attention of someone who understands from a clinical point of view how human behavior works in crisis situations.

In finding someone to talk to about your life as a caregiver, there are a number of issues to consider, such as when you should actually begin therapy, the different types of therapists that are available, and where to find the one you need. You will also need to have some idea of what the process involves and what you can expect from the whole experience.

At what point should you seek professional counseling? Simply stated, you should seek it when you have reached your breaking point. When is that? It varies, of course, from one person to another, but you can consider having reached it when your normal stress level reaches a level of abnormal distress, when your negative feelings of anger and depression overwhelm your impulse to provide for your spouse's welfare, and when your standard support system no longer works for you and you want *out* of your life as a caregiver. You need help when you lose your workable perspective and are out of control, and you no longer care for your spouse in any real sense of the word.

A crisis situation that requires professional intervention can occur in any type of long-term illness or disease. A Maryland psychiatrist describes how it happens in the case of head injury:

> The real trouble (for the caregiver) starts a couple of years after the traumatic event, when the victim doesn't get better and the healthy spouse begins to see what he or she is in for. Feelings start to turn in on themselves. The caregiver becomes bitter and depressed, and the quality of care is affected. At that point I begin to focus my attention away from the patient to the caregiver. It can take a lot of time to draw them out again.

If your feelings about spousal support are turning in on you *at the expense* of your partner's health and welfare, whether he or she has suffered a head injury or is living with the effects of stroke or triple bypass surgery or other illness or disease, you may need professional care to help you put things back into the workable perspective you need to be an effective caregiver again. If and when you realize this, don't wait; start looking for help immediately.

Types of Counseling

What kinds of help are available and does everyone who needs help need a psychiatrist? There are several varieties of professional counseling available, all falling under the general heading of psychotherapy. No, not everyone needs a psychiatrist. A psychiatrist is a medical doctor who specializes in the treatment and prevention of serious mental and emotional disorders, including psychosis and neurosis, which may hinder or cause a major breakdown in a person's ability to function, not only in stress situations but in society as a whole. You need a psychiatrist if your spouse's illness has impaired you to this extent, or if you cannot effectively care for your spouse without medication. Many people go to psychiatrists with lesser problems, but it is not always prudent or necessary.

You may want to consider a clinical psychologist for help. Clinical psychologists are not physicians, but they do have advanced degrees and training in the study of human behavior. Unlike psychiatrists, who specialize in mental illness and disease, clinical psychologists tend to focus more on what is "normal" in the way we act with one another. While you may find this less intimidating than the psychiatric approach, bear in mind that clinical psychologists are known to give many tests to discover just how "normal" people are, and that may not be what you are looking for either. See a clinical psychologist if you wish to determine what *is* normal in your life and how you can apply that to your life as a caregiving spouse.

If you want to restrict professional intervention to helping you adjust to the problems you face as a caregiver, you may benefit more from counseling by settling for less—not in abilities or clinical experience but by way of time and expense. Psychiatric nurses, social workers, and pastoral counselors represent this level of therapy. Psychiatric nurses and social workers hold advanced degrees, are licensed by the state, and have extensive experience in their respective fields of competence. They specialize in working in troubled family situations. They are not as concerned with uncovering and correcting pathological behavior as they are with the practical aspects of helping persons adjust to difficult family situations. Pastoral counselors are usually ordained clergypersons who have seminary degrees and advanced training through courses in clinical pastoral education and supervision of their counseling activities. Many are accredited by the American Association of Pastoral Counselors. Pastoral counselors do much the same thing as their professional counterparts but are more likely to place family relationships and responsibilities in a spiritual context. If you see the problems you encounter in your caregiving role as personal faith issues, a pastoral counselor or psychotherapist can help clarify your understanding of that role as a test of what your beliefs are, as a means of expanding your relationship with God, or as a way of deepening the love you share with your partner.

Deciding what kind of help you need depends largely on how demoralized and incapacitated you feel in meeting your caregiving responsibilities. It also depends, as in the case of most health care services, on how much the help costs. As a general rule, the farther up the training scale the more expensive the treatment. Psychiatric care is considered a medical expense by most insurance companies. Most policies will cover at least part of these services. Psychologists, psychiatric nurses who are state- and board-certified, and licensed clinical social workers (LCSWs) are also eligible for insurance benefits in most cases but probably require a medical referral. Unfortunately, pastoral counseling services are usually excluded from most insurance policies at the present time, but many pastoral counselors and agencies will work on a sliding fee scale.

Where to Find Counselors

Once you have made the decision that you need professional help as a caregiving spouse, where do you go to find it? Again, the best source of information about this kind of help is your family physician or the social worker at your hospital, both of whom can make a referral. You may also consult your minister, priest, or rabbi. If they have had some formal training in pastoral care, they will probably recognize the degree of difficulty you are experiencing in caring for your spouse and make the appropriate recommendation. You can talk with friends whose judgment you trust and who have been in counseling themselves. If they are "satisfied customers" of some particular therapist, you may want to give that person a try. You can also contact the psychology departments or counseling centers of local colleges and universities, where staff members may be available for private consultation. In most larger communities there are referral agencies for all types of social services, including counseling. These agencies usually have the name, number, and speciality of subscribing therapists available in your area. If all else fails, try the Yellow Pages. It's a bit risky to go this route, since you do not know what you are getting into, but at least you will have a list of names and agencies in front of you in the order of their specialty.

What Therapy Should Do for You

Once you have sought out and found the right source of individual help for yourself, what should you expect from your therapeutic experience? You should feel better about yourself and able to do a better job in your role as a caregiving spouse. You should expect help with getting through your crisis of commitment and not feel so guilty about the desire to shirk your responsibilities. Expect help in claiming your right to a life and an identity apart from your caregiving duties, in reclaiming that workable perspective that you must have when you are "on the job."

Leonard Diller, a rehabilitative psychologist at the Rusk Institute in New York City, feels that the object of individual therapy for the caregiving spouse is to keep that perspective in the form of a realistic assessment of the limits of the patient's abilities to care for his or her own needs. Dr. Diller, who works with the families of chronically ill patients at the Rusk Institute, says:

> The well spouse needs to realize that the illness will never fully go away. Some effects are treatable, but not curable; they are the result of permanent loss of function. You must learn to live with the changes caused by the illness by developing a whole new gestalt or sense of what the patient can or cannot do.

To do this, Dr. Diller believes that caregivers must learn to recognize the significant steps that their spouses take in their journey toward recovery. These steps serve as markers along the way that define the caregiver's limits in responding to the spouse's need for support and the spouse's limits in supporting himself or herself in any given point in the rehabilitation process. Each marker further defines the caregiver/caretaker relationship as well. As a caregiver you have the responsibility to support your spouse beyond his or her ability to fully recover from the illness, but you also have the right to refrain from caring for your spouse when you recognize that it is beyond your ability or would be personally harmful for you to do so. You have the right to your own integrity and self-respect within your caregiving relationship. You also have the right to ask for help in maintaining it. To affirm this is to place your responsibilities as a caregiver into what Dr. Diller calls a gestalt, or holistic perspective, which obviously includes care and support for yourself as well as your spouse.

What else should you expect from therapy? Merle McCann, a Baltimore psychiatrist who works with AIDS patients, believes that caregivers deserve honest and practical advice as much as profound clinical insight in caring for a chronically ill or dying patient. He agrees that a medical crisis is not an opportunity to examine family pathology and suggests that the time could be better spent building a quality relationship between patient and caregiver:

> So often the constant demands of treating an illness overshadows its meaning for the caregiver and patient. One is so busy caring and the other is so busy being cared for that neither has time to consider what is going on between them.

Dr. McCann gives this advice to the caregiver:

> Stop and rest from your duties—even when the impulse to go on is strong. If you're not doing enough, realize that you never can do enough and try to focus your attention on how the illness has changed and enriched your lives together—even if the time is short.

In short, Dr. McCann is saying that it makes sense to make the best of a bad situation, and this is a legitimate goal of therapy.

Paulette Scott, a clinical social worker and pastoral counselor, feels the most important help a therapist can provide caregivers is the permission and opportunity to be simply themselves.

> People can become someone else when they become caregivers. They lose themselves in their work. At best they overlook their own needs for nurture and support; at worst they are fooling them-

selves into thinking they are omnipotent, that they can and should do everything for their loved ones.

Paulette has often asked me what I celebrate in my life— apart from my love and devotion as a caregiver. Her point is that all caregiving spouses *have* another life to celebrate, a life in which we are all free to be ourselves— to laugh, to be thankful over the fact of our own existence, and to respect our own individual integrity.

These sentiments reflect a very healthy attitude for caregiving spouses to adopt and are further expressed in the words of an anonymous poem called "Let Go," which was sent to me while doing research for this book:

> Let go. . . .
>
> To "let go" does not mean to stop caring, it means I can't always do it for someone else.
>
> To "let go" is to admit powerlessness, which means the outcome is not in my hands.
>
> To "let go" is not always to care for them, but also to care about myself.
>
> To "let go" is not to regret the past, but to grow and live for the future.
>
> To "let go" is to fear less, and love more.

If professional therapy does anything for you as a caregiving spouse, it ought to help you feel better by making you less afraid to claim your right to a life of your own. It should also make you a better caregiver by helping you see that you have not just the obligation but the right to let go, "to fear less, and love more." If you can find someone to help you make that choice successfully, you will have received more than you may have expected from an individual therapeutic experience.

10

Counting the Cost

As a veteran caregiver you know how serious illness can disrupt or even devastate a marriage. You know the initial shock it can produce, the major upheaval it causes in a marital relationship, and the often bitter feelings it leaves behind. You know all this from your own experience, and yet you have learned to cope with and even overcome some of the obstacles that blocked your way. But now, just as it seems you have gotten a handle on your situation, you are faced with still another major issue in your spouse's critical or chronic illness: Who is going to pay for it?

Medical care is frightfully expensive. Less than a month after Jackie's stroke I received two statements from the hospital where she was in intensive care. I opened one, looked at the bottom line for the amount due as the patient's liability, and saw a figure of $106,000! Fortunately, I found the second statement was a continuation of the first, and the amount for which we were liable was reduced to a mere $133. When I recovered from the shock I gladly paid what we actually owed, but the point was made. Medical costs have skyrocketed in our society today, and someone has to pay them.

No doubt at this point in the course of your spouse's illness you have already had to contend with the costs of medical care. You have dealt with hospital charges and doctors' bills and prescriptions and therapy costs and everything else it takes to make your husband or wife well again. But, how much do you really know about what you are doing? We live in a period of major change in health care funding. How do these changes affect your situation? How can your and your spouse afford this illness?

As a caregiver you must be both vigilant and informed in your pursuit of health care that is as cost effective as it is medically sound. Catastrophic illness costs tens and often hundreds of thousands of dollars to treat today, and the costs of chronic illness, as you may well know, are open-ended. You need to know what you are doing in counting the cost of medical care, lest you and your spouse both fall victim to the crippling expenses of illness or disease.

In this chapter, we will look at the different kinds of financial support available to cover the costs of medical expenses today, along with ways to go about obtaining the proper coverage for your present and future medical needs. We will also consider some practical advice on maximizing your benefits while minimizing your expenses, advice on how to make sure you receive all the benefits you pay for and deserve.

Medical Insurance

In lieu of a comprehensive national health program such as exists in Canada or the United Kingdom, medical insurance in the United States is a hybrid combination of privately owned and federally funded programs. You probably know from your own experience that this arrangement is far from perfect, but since it is all we have you will need to make it work for you as best you can.

Major insurance companies that offer life, home, automobile, and casualty insurance in most states will usually offer medical insurance as well. Policies vary in cost and coverage and are usually offered through an employer on a group basis in order to provide the maximum amount of coverage for the least cost. Some other employers are self-insured; they have established their own medical plans funded by employer and employee contributions.

Blue Cross

The most widely used private insurance program in America is the Blue Cross/Blue Shield network, operating in all fifty states. Blue Cross/Blue Shield, or the "Blues" as it is sometimes referred to, is a comprehensive program of medical coverage that is available to almost everyone who can pay for it. You may obtain insurance on an individual or group basis, ranging from a basic plan to those with higher levels of coverage, whether you are self-employed or whether you work for a large company. Basic coverage is just what it implies; you receive minimum protection against hospital costs and physicians' fees at the least possible cost to you. Basic coverage includes higher deductibles (the amount you pay for medical services before benefits are available) and higher coinsurance requirements (the amount you pay for services after the deductible has been met and benefits have been provided to you). Basic coverage may also limit the total amount of insurance available for the life of the policy. As you move up the scale toward higher levels of coverage, deductibles and coinsurance requirements decrease and your options for obtaining different kinds of insurance service become more numerous. Although individual and group plans vary from state to state, many will offer additional services according to your needs, including coverage for catastrophic illness, organ transplants, nursing home care, prescription drugs, dental and vision plans, extended inpatient and outpatient psychiatric services, and coverage for several kinds of therapy.

In recent years health care providers, including Blue Cross/Blue Shield, have moved into the area of prepaid health care plans in order to contain burgeoning costs while still offering the same levels of medical care to their subscribers. These plans, commonly known as Competitive Medical Plans (CMPs) or Health Maintenance Organizations (HMOs), offer a full range of health care services to their members in exchange for a monthly fixed fee. They are preferable to other plans because they are smaller, better contained and organized than huge industrial or statewide programs, and therefore less expensive to operate. Services are provided only to members who receive care at their local hospital or clinics located in the community. Physicians and other medical professionals are paid by the plan to provide services, often at a comparatively modest rate, in exchange for a steady flow of patients who are plan members. It is a mutually beneficial arrangement; members are assured of care and doctors are assured of work. The only disadvantage of such a plan is that a member of a particular HMO or CMP may not always receive care in another plan without paying for it as an out-of-pocket expense. That can present problems if you are out of your service area and you or your spouse need immediate medical attention.

Blue Cross/Blue Shield, however, is a membership organization made up of patient subscribers and health care providers. All subscribers agree to pay a certain monthly premium for services; all providers agree to accept a standard fee, usually referred to as a customary or prevailing or reasonable charge. If you receive medical care from a licensed health care professional who is not part of the Blue Cross/Blue Shield network, you will only be reimbursed for the customary charge for the given medical service; you may be responsible for paying any extra charges on your own. Also, when traveling out of state as a Blue Cross subscriber, while you are still covered for medical care should you need it, you may have to pay for some or all of your medical expenses and be reimbursed by your plan at a later date after you return home.

Medicare

The closest thing to a national health care plan in this country is Medicare. Medicare is a federally funded health insurance program for people sixty-five and over and certain other persons who are disabled. It is administered by the Department of Health and Human Services and the Social Security Administration. Benefits are divided into two parts: Hospital Insurance and Medical Insurance. Part A, Hospital Insurance, covers inpatient hospital care and some skilled nursing-home care, home health care, and hospice care. Part B, Medical Insurance, covers doctors' fees, special practitioners' services, and outpatient medical service and supplies.

As of 1990, the benefits under Part A for inpatient hospital services included coverage for semiprivate rooms, intensive and coronary care, medication, laboratory and rehabilitation services, and all medical supplies and equipment for up to ninety days during each benefit period. "Benefit period" is a term used to measure the length of time a Medicare recipient is eligible to use hospital insurance. It starts the first day a person enters a hospital or nursing home and ends sixty days after discharge.

Home health services covered by Part A include part-time skilled nursing care, physical, speech, and occupational therapy, and medical supplies and equipment up to 80 percent of their approved cost. Hospice care includes both home and inpatient nursing care for the terminally ill in addition to homemaking and counseling services for the patient's family.

Medicare coverage under Part B, medical insurance, includes most inpatient services provided by a physician, including surgery, diagnostic tests and procedures, radiology and X rays, and psychiatric treatment. It also helps to pay for treatment given by other medical professionals such as podiatrists, optometrists, chiropractors, and clinical psychologists. Outpatient services covered by medical insurance include emergency room treatment, laboratory tests, certain home health care, rehabilitation services, and most medical equipment that your spouse would need at home.

Medicare is as close to a comprehensive medical insurance program as we have in our society today. If you and your husband or wife are covered under Medicare you are aware of the many services it provides. You may also be aware, however, of the deductible and coinsurance amounts that you have to pay when you submit a claim, which should remind you that Medicare was never designed to meet all your hospital or medical needs. You should carry supplemental or "Medigap" insurance that is specifically designed to cover those health care expenses not covered by Medicare. Of particular importance is coverage for catastrophic illness, which Medicare sought to insure through the Catastrophic Coverage Act of 1988. The act was repealed in 1990, and Medicare recipients must once again find this insurance through private supplemental programs. Since your spouse may have suffered an illness that could qualify as catastrophic, you know how important it is to have this type of coverage.

Detailed information about Medicare benefits and how the program works is available through publications of the Health Care Financing Administration of the Department of Human Services. Information is also available through your local Social Security office and probably through the employee benefit office of your or your spouse's place of employment.

Medicaid

Medicaid is an additional public health care program. Often confused with Medicare, it operates on the state level to provide medical assistance more to persons who are indigent rather than to those persons who are retired or disabled. Medicaid provides hospital and medical care for those persons whose financial resources have been depleted by the expense of a critical or chronic illness. In most states married persons in need of medical care can qualify for Medicaid if their total assets, except for home and personal possessions, are under $3,000 and their combined income is under $425 per month. At that level, and if all other eligibility requirements have been met, most medical services are available on a fully funded basis. There are no copayments or deductibles with Medicaid, nor are the procedures for receiving Medicaid benefits as complicated as they are with Medicare. If you and your spouse find that, because of chronic illness, your current insurance benefits and savings are exhausted and there is still no end in sight to your increasing medical expenses, you may qualify for Medicaid. Eligibility requirements and a list of the health care services that are available to you can be obtained through the social service agency of the local municipality in which you live.

Other Possibilities

There may be still other sources of financial support to help pay the costs associated with your spouse's critical or chronic illness.

We spoke about vocational rehabilitation benefits in chapter 7 and mentioned that, in addition to providing employment training and placement, vocational rehabilitation can furnish clients with cost-of-living allowances as part of the individual rehabilitation plan. Disability benefits may also be available to you through Social Security, Worker's Compensation, or even the Veterans Administration. If your spouse has worked and paid into Social Security for a certain number of consecutive quarters and meets the established criteria for disability, he or she will be eligible to receive disability benefits after a five-month waiting period. Contact your local Social Security office for additional details. If your spouse's illness or disease is a result of a job-related injury, he or she may be eligible for Worker's Compensation benefits. Your own attorney or one who specializes in Worker's Compensation can help you with your case. If your spouse is a military veteran, he or she may be eligible for medical and rehabilitative services as part of the life-long veterans' benefits. Contact your local VA office or medical center for more information on the benefits and services your spouse may need.

Managing Your Money

Adequate medical insurance is critical to seeing your way through any medical emergency today, but regardless of how or where you find coverage for your spouse's illness there are always some practical things you can do to manage your own financial situation and get the most out of the benefits and services that you pay for in your insurance premiums.

The first thing you can do is learn to manage your money more carefully. We live in a society where we are encouraged to spend and not save, to be in debt and not out of it. For couples who are already in debt, a spouse's major illness can be a financial disaster. Such people owe thousands of dollars in medical bills they cannot pay and may lose their credit rating; in one case I was told about, a family lost its home due to the expenses of one single illness. A word that comes to mind here in counting the costs of illness and disease is "thrift," and every caregiver I have met since I became one myself has had to practice it.

A caregiving wife wrote to me from Ontario, Canada, about how she coped with expenses following her husband's stroke:

> Hal was sixty-four when our world flew apart five years ago. . . . We had some money saved, but it's mostly gone now. Not being affluent anyway I've had to manage quite carefully, and I've learned a lot in

the do-it-yourself category. Want me to come and mortar your house, or advise you on a list of subjects that were never my cup of tea? . . . It's very frustrating, but you need to learn to make do and hope that sometime good fortune will appear in your life.

The short- and long-term financial effects of critical and chronic illness can cause a major upheaval in how you budget your family income. If you were spending most of it before your spouse's illness, you probably experienced a serious financial bind after it occurred. In our case, because Jackie and I both worked, our family income was permanently reduced by one third even after her disability and retirement benefits began. Although our expenses have fortunately remained the same, it took some innovative financial adjustment over the years to compensate for our loss, and some of our plans for the future have had to be shelved for a while. No doubt you will have to deal with similar budget limitations in your family. Be prepared to establish some new priorities on how and where you spend your money. Your family's clothing, entertainment, and travel allowances, your educational plans for your children, even the food budget may have to be modified in order to provide for expected and unexpected medical expenses that are simply not covered no matter how good your insurance is.

In planning for your financial future, talk to your accountant or lawyer about decisions you need to make. Talk to other caregiving spouses in your support group or circle of friends who have had to confront similar financial problems. Learn from their experiences—their successes and their mistakes. To avoid mistakes consider the services of a financial planner who specializes in helping people organize their assets to their maximum advantage. A financial planner is not a broker, banker, accountant, attorney, or even an insurance agent, but rather a combination of all of them who helps you review your assets, tells you how to invest them and make money, and how to save money in taxes and fees, all in accord with the law. Financial planners do not handle your money for you; they simply advise you on how to handle it yourself. Get the names of good financial planners from persons you know and trust, such as your banker or your attorney, or from friends who have used their services in the past. Once you have found one you like, ask for and check out references. If possible, make sure that the person is registered with an accredited organization, such as the International Association for Financial Planning, located in Atlanta, Georgia. Organizations like these list the names of certified financial planners in your area and provide extensive information on how the planning process works and how much it will cost.

Some additional things you can do to cut down on your medical expenses and manage your finances more effectively include working with doctors and other health care providers who are members of your particular health care plan and learning to negotiate fees charged by those who are not. The nature of your spouse's illness will determine how much latitude you have in choosing a physician to treat it. If your spouse's medical condition is chronic, you have sufficient time to make sure that the physicians, therapists, and home health care workers you choose accept the reasonable and customary fees that your insurance company assigns to particular medical procedures and services. In emergency or critical situations, however, your options may be limited and the doctor who takes your case may not accept assignment, in which case you may have to make up the difference between what your insurance company pays you and what you must pay the doctor. If that difference is a significant one, you would do well to try to reduce the fee through negotiation. We live in a competitive society where most things are negotiable; for better or worse, that includes health care. Doctor's fees are not carved in granite, and most physicians are reasonable and conscientious people. The chances are if you can demonstrate that a particular charge for medical treatment is more than you can reasonably afford, it will be reduced to a more manageable level. Do not be afraid to bargain. Keep in mind that the intent of your negotiation is to arrive at a figure that you can afford to pay and the doctor is willing to accept as a just compensation for his or her services. The same thing also applies to other health care providers such as therapists, private duty nurses, medical supply and equipment houses, and pharmacists. If you contract for a set amount of hours, you may be able to get a reduced rate for therapy or nursing care. In the same way, if you know you will need and are willing to agree in advance to buy large quantities of medical supplies or medication from a single supplier, you may get a significant discount on your purchase. Things are cheaper by the dozen, and those things include health care items.

Another bit of practical information on counting the costs of health care concerns purchasing generic drugs whenever you can in place of the more expensive name-brand ones. Most insurance companies with drug prescription programs do this routinely as a cost-saving measure, and you should also. Your doctor will make sure that the generic drugs work as well as the "real thing" and help you avoid those that do not. Also, when paying doctor and hospital bills make sure you know what you are being billed for and that you are not overpaying your share of the cost of your spouse's medical care. If necessary, request that the bills be itemized. Check them against the insurance statements. Be persistent and ask questions about all the technical jargon that is on the statements. All of it eventually translates into money you owe, so before you pay you should understand the translation.

Finally, when counting the cost of your spouse's critical or chronic illness, learn to expect the unexpected. Expect obstacles in your way when applying for the benefits described in this chapter and time delays in being

approved for them. Expect the confusion that is part of
an inquiry with an insurance company for reimburse-
ment of a medical expense. Be prepared to hear the
all-too-familiar response, "I'm sorry, but our computer is
down and we can't help you until tomorrow." Look for
trouble with your credit rating if you are habitually unable to pay your bills on time. Expect the unexpected in
the form of charges for your spouse's medical care that
show up one or two or even six months after the services
were provided; services that either fall through the
cracks in your insurance coverage or that you are just too
exhausted to argue about any longer and the path of least
resistance is simply to pay up on your own and forget
about them.

Meeting the costs of your spouse's illness can become
a test of wills, and sometimes the system wins and you
will have to pay. Keep in mind, however, as you count
the costs of your partner's medical care, that in the long
run the system will work to bring your husband or wife
back to the health and vitality he or she enjoyed before
being taken ill. In the long run that is your goal—whatever the cost may be.

11

When Illness Ends in Death

Everything we have covered on spousal support so far in this book is based on the premise that your caregiving efforts will lead to your spouse's recovery from illness, or at least that both of you will learn to live with the effects of your husband or wife's condition on a long-term or even permanent basis. It would be grossly unfair to many caregivers, however, to say that with the right kind of care every illness and disease passes from the critical stage to the curative or to deny the fact that there are many illnesses and caregiving situations for which there is no cure or happy ending.

How do you deal with an illness that is terminal? What kind of care do you give to your spouse when each of you knows that, no matter what you do, your love, commitment, and energy can never bring about a return to health?

Death is always a shock to us; it is an unwelcome visitor, whether sudden or anticipated. The death of a spouse due to sudden illness or injury brings its own set of consequences: the numbness and pain, the element of unexpected and unwelcome surprise, great emotional and intellectual confusion, and a lack of preparation to deal with the more practical consequences of our loss. Anticipated death, however ("dying after a long illness" as it is euphemistically described in the obituary columns of local newspapers), seems to mask the impact of our loss. Because it is expected, or even welcomed in some cases, we are more apt to deal with its consequences, but only after we and our spouses have endured a long period of emotional suffering and preparation.

In this chapter we will look at the eventuality of death as a natural conclusion to critical and chronic illness, and we will consider ways in which you can minimize the impact of your loss. Specifically, we will consider how both you and your mate can prepare for and accept death as a natural and fitting conclusion to your life together and how you can go on living with the knowledge that as a partner in marriage you did all that you could as well as you could to love and care for your spouse when his or her life literally depended on you.

Janet and Sam were married for twenty-one years. For all their married life they lived in a suburb of Washington, D.C. Janet is a forty-two-year-old government worker; Sam taught industrial arts at a local high school for most of his professional career and was appointed department chair in 1981. Early in 1984 Sam began experiencing severe headaches and double vision. After a thorough neurological examination it was discovered that he was suffering from a meningioma, a slow-growing nonmalignant brain tumor. Surgery was performed in May of that year, after which the neurosurgeon assured Sam and Janet that, while he could not get it all, enough of the tumor was removed so that its effects would not be felt again until Sam was an old man, when he would "probably die from something else." Unfortunately, the tumor grew back within the year to a point where it was immediately life-threatening. Sam underwent three months of daily radiation, which failed to shrink the tumor, and was given the choice of a second surgery or chemotherapy as the next option for treatment. He chose an eight-month course of chemotherapy, during which time, with Janet's help, he went back to work and tried to resume a normal family and social life as best he could.

In early 1986 while driving to his doctor's office for a checkup Sam suffered a seizure, had an accident, and totaled his car. He was uninjured, but he began to show the first permanent signs of his illness after the seizure, including memory loss, mental confusion, and an overall lack of awareness. It was apparent that the chemotherapy was not working, and the effects of the illness grew with the frequency and intensity of his seizures. Sam became increasingly immobilized and dependent on Janet, who took a temporary leave of absence from her job to become her husband's full-time caregiver. He had to retire from his job on a medical disability and remained at home, where he became increasingly argumentative and antisocial and threatened Janet with bodily harm on several occasions. As a last resort the doctors suggested a second surgery, which was performed in the summer of 1986. Because the tumor had enlarged and attached itself to Sam's brain to the extent that it could not be removed, the surgery was unsuccessful and the doctors concluded nothing more could be done. Sam's condition continued to deteriorate over the next few months, to the point where Janet could no longer care for him at home. He entered a nearby hospice in the fall of that year and died six weeks later, after slipping into a coma, with Janet, a hospice nurse, and a priest at his bedside.

I spoke with Janet at length about the meaning of her husband's illness and death for her. They were comparatively young when Sam was taken ill and he was much too young by anyone's standards to die. Janet had all the responsibilities and obstacles to face as a caregiving wife that we have talked about elsewhere in this book, and with them all came the added emotional burden of knowing that in the end Sam was going to lose the battle and she was going to lose him. Now that Janet was alone,

what purpose could be served by Sam's death? Here are
some of her responses.

> It takes me back whenever I think of losing Sam,
> even after three years. I'd like to forget a lot of the
> experiences, but what I do remember was hell on
> wheels. . . . At first you want to deny how serious it
> is; you think your husband will get better, and will
> still do things like fix the electric toaster or do the
> taxes, but after a few costly mistakes you have to face
> facts. . . . I got very angry with the doctors for not
> knowing how to save his life, with our friends for
> deserting us. . . . I was left alone to pick up the pieces.
> . . . Toward the end, though, I had to let the anger
> go in order to let Sam go. He led the fight against the
> illness, and when he started to give up I did too.
> . . .
>
> What did I learn from this? I learned that suffering
> is very real and personal, but I have the ability to
> endure it. I also learned that I could give up the
> thing I loved more than anything in my life and still
> survive. Most married people don't know that.

Janet endured the tragic loss of her husband. Today
she leads a full life and belongs to a support group in
which she helps other caregiving spouses deal with the
death of their marriage partners. I believe that what she
says is true—most married couples who are facing terminal illness in their lives together do not know that the
surviving spouse can go on alone successfully. If you are
a caregiver whose spouse is dying and you are wondering
how you will survive, there are some things you both can
do to ease the pain of separation and ensure your future
welfare when you are finally left alone.

Facing Reality

To begin with, it would be most helpful to each of you
to try and face the truth together. Most couples when

confronted by a terminal illness will deal with its impact at varying stages, depending on who knows what or who hears the news first. A woman with heart disease may know that she has very little time to live but is afraid to say anything for fear of upsetting her husband, who is trying so hard to help her get well. Or a wife may be told that her husband will soon die from complications following a stroke, and she is naturally inclined to protect him from this news as long as possible. Or a husband who is aware that his wife will succumb to breast cancer will want to put off telling her until the "right" time comes along. In all these situations it is important for couples to realize that the fatal outcome of a particular illness cannot be denied indefinitely, and it is doubly important that they use their remaining time together as productively as possible. In your own situation you should have the courage and take the time to admit the reality of death into your lives and try as best you can to talk with each other about the end that is waiting to happen. Your spouse is about to lose her or his life and you are going to lose your way of life—as a caregiver and as a marriage partner.

This is an indescribably sad time in your relationship together, but it is also a momentous opportunity. It is an opportunity to face your loss together, to go through the process of anticipatory grief, as Elisabeth Kubler-Ross describes it, where you unite in your feelings of shock and disbelief and anger over the loss that is to come and finally arrive together at that point where each of you is able to accept your separation with equanimity and peace. It is a time to remember and celebrate your past, to tie up loose ends and unfinished business, a time to give and get permission to let go of each other, knowing that your life together was good—even if it was not long enough.

If you and your spouse are able to talk about the ultimate reality of death with each other, it follows that you should also discuss its more secular aspects as a means of preparation and acceptance. Specifically, you ought to take the time to make appropriate funeral and burial arrangements, to attend to necessary business affairs, and to make sure that you understand all the legal matters in your life together, including your spouse's feelings about being kept alive on life-support systems should he or she become comatose or permanently unconscious.

Funeral Arrangements

There is a trend today toward preplanning funerals—making arrangements before death occurs. This is a good idea even if your spouse is terminally ill and death is imminent. It gives the dying person the opportunity to participate actively in the ritual of departure—to plan the funeral service or decide on viewing and burial arrangements if he or she wishes. It avoids the pain and pressure of your having to do all this alone after your partner is gone and you are dealing with your primary feelings of loss and grief. Most funeral directors offer preplanning services and will be happy to help you at your convenience.

Financial Affairs

Taking care of business in the event of a fatal illness means that as a surviving spouse you will be protected by those assets you now share. Talk *now* with your accountant or financial planner in order to insure your financial future. Your discussion should include what will happen to real property, bank accounts, stocks, bonds, and any other assets that are in your spouse's name. You may wish to consider joint ownership, if that is not the case already, or putting them in your name only if your spouse feels this is appropriate, in order to preserve your legal claim to these assets when death occurs. In any case, your consultation should be frank and inclusive, and its end result should guarantee your financial security as far into the future as possible.

Legal Matters

Getting your joint legal affairs in order obviously includes additional consultation with your attorney and the proper execution of a *will.* A will stipulates how a person wishes to divide his or her assets at the time of death. Almost everyone should have a will, yet the fact is that a large percentage of people in our society die intestate—without a will. Do not let your mate be one of them. There is no legal guarantee that as a surviving spouse you will automatically inherit the estate. Laws in the distribution of estate assets vary from one state to another, and it is possible that without a will you could receive as little as one half of what you and your spouse built up over the course of your married life. Do not let that happen to you. Talk to your attorney with your spouse about estate planning. If you do not have an attorney, contact your local bar association for a referral. Making a will or updating the one you have is a relatively easy and inexpensive legal procedure that is vitally important to your future welfare.

Another legal instrument that may be vital to your immediate welfare is a *power of attorney.* If your spouse is terminally ill it may be wise for him or her to give you the right to make legal decisions without his or her expressed permission or approval. This is especially important if your spouse's assets (on which you must depend) are in his or her name only or held in joint ownership without right of survivorship. A power of attorney in these circumstances gives you some control over your own life as you continue to care for your husband or wife and as you look toward the time when you will have to manage on your own.

If you do not have power of attorney and your spouse's condition has deteriorated to the point where he or she is no longer competent to give it, you may have to go to court to file for *legal guardian* or *conservatorship* over the person and property of your spouse. In such circumstances the court appoints you as your spouse's guardian and gives you permission to manage your spouse's affairs. This is a lengthy, complicated, and often expensive procedure, involving hearings, investigations of your character, annual fiduciary reports, and so forth. Having gone through it myself in the course of my wife's illness, I am convinced that you should be as prepared as possible in all legal matters pertaining to fatal illness.

Two other documents that should be considered here as part of your defense against the devastating effects of terminal illness are living wills and durable powers of attorney for health care. Known in legal terms as advance directives, they can provide you and your spouse with ultimate control over the course of treatment for illness or disease, should she or he ever become comatose or permanently unconscious. *Living wills* are the personal declarations of individuals, usually invoked by a proxy in the final stages of a terminal illness when a patient is mentally incapacitated or unconscious, specifying what treatment procedures they want or do not want used to sustain their life. These procedures (or "heroic measures," as they are often called) include things like cardiopulmonary resuscitation (CPR), respiratory therapy, antibiotics, experimental treatment or surgery, and, in some cases, the continuation of food and water. *Durable powers of attorney for health care* allow an individual to name another person to act as agent in making decisions about treatment for terminal illness, should the patient become personally unable to do so. The powers given to an agent in this document can range from action that must be taken under a specific set of medical circumstances to giving the agent free rein in making decisions about the patient's health care.

At the time of this writing only forty states have passed living will statutes in our country, and I have been told of more than one situation in which medical institutions such as hospitals and nursing homes have refused to honor living wills when family members or proxies tried to invoke them. Much of the reservations and confusion about a person's right to refuse life-sustaining medical treatment is bound up in what has become the "right-to-die" movement in our society. The debate over who has the right to live versus the right to die, and under what circumstances that decision may be made, is fraught with many legal and moral considerations.

In June of 1990 the Supreme Court issued a ruling that such a decision may not be made at all unless there is "clear and convincing evidence" of a person's prior wishes to have life-sustaining procedures either withheld or withdrawn if he or she were terminally ill or permanently unconscious. In a case involving the State of Missouri and the family of Nancy Beth Cruzan, a thirty-two-year-old woman who had been in a persistent vegetative state since a 1983 car crash, the court said that without such evidence a state, and presumably the hospitals and nursing homes within its bounds, was under no legal obligation to permit the removal of life-support systems on the basis of a family's sole claim that the patient would have wanted it that way. Implicit in its ruling, however, was the recognition of living wills and durable powers of attorney for health care as documentary evidence of a person's right to refuse all life-sustaining procedures in the event of imminent death.

The legal debate still goes on from state to state, but current wisdom suggests that the best protection you can have against unwanted and unnecessary life-sustaining procedures intruding into your own situation is to have both a living will *and* a durable power of attorney for health care. These documents are readily obtainable through your state and local health care agencies, private organizations such as the Society for the Right to Die (see Resources at the back of this book for their address), or your local bar association, to name a few. You do not need an attorney to execute either of them, although they must be properly witnessed and should be notarized as an added precaution, especially if you should move to

another state. The wording of living wills and durable
powers of attorney for health care vary from state to
state, so you must be sure that you conform to your state
statutes. Samples of those developed for use in Maryland
are included under Resources for your examination.

If your spouse is terminally ill and unable to speak, and
through the execution of a living will or durable power
of attorney you are the proxy or agent, you may be considering whether or not to remove your spouse's life-
support systems or withhold them altogether. If this is
the case, what are some of the moral issues involved and
how can you best make your decision?

While I was neither my wife's proxy nor agent because
we did not have a living will or a medical power of attorney in force, I was faced with making this same decision
in the course of her illness in the spring of 1986. Jackie's
stroke was the result of an intercerebral and subarach-
noid hemorrhage. From the moment her condition was
first diagnosed I was given virtually no hope there would
be any kind of recovery; the damage to the brain was
thought to have been too massive and irreversible. On
the fortieth day of her stroke, while Jackie was still in a
deep coma, after consulting at length with our children
and Jackie's doctor, who told me that Jackie might live
for years in a persistent vegetative state, I made the
decision, as her husband and legal guardian, to seek permission from the court to remove Jackie from her life
support systems.

As the drama unfolded, the judge decided to stay the
decision, pending further investigation of legal prece-
dent in our case, and in the interim Jackie miraculously
awoke from her coma and began a long recovery from
her stroke. Yet I remain convinced that my decision to
let her go was a fundamentally moral one because I had
her best interests in mind at the time I made it. Though
her coma prevented her from experiencing physical
pain, I saw her ordeal as a growing insult to her dignity
and her spirit, and I knew her suffering would have been

intolerable to her if she were actually aware of her condition. I also still believe that an obligation to cure or sustain a person's life in the face of an incurable illness ceases when we can no longer contribute to the ability to live a purposeful life, a life striving toward wholeness and personal fulfillment. Jackie's life was no longer demonstrating that purpose. She was not living a meaningful life. Thus I made my decision.

If you are faced with a similar decision about the life of your terminally or incurably ill spouse, how can you make it in good conscience and reasonable certainty that you are doing the right thing? There are a number of factors to take into consideration, such as your spouse's medical condition (have all possible options for recovery been exhausted?) and personal feelings (would your spouse want to remain on life supports indefinitely?), and of course you should be clear in your own feelings about the right to live or die. But the final consideration in making your decision ought to be this: If the medical condition and prognosis is so uniformly poor that the continuation of life by artificial means is of *no conceivable benefit to your spouse,* it is appropriate to allow her or him to die—in mercy and dignity. In the final analysis, it is your spouse's own ability to recapture a lost identity and self-worth that determines the future course of her or his life. If your spouse lacks the strength and resolve to do this, it is morally right in my judgment to see that life come to a fitting and timely end.

Affirming Life

Within the Judeo-Christian heritage, death holds both a temporal and a spiritual importance. In its most literal sense, death is the obvious and often painful ending of a person's life. A life that was once shared in marriage, family, and friendship is no more. Now comes separation, mourning, and loss, and eventually understanding and acceptance. It is in these latter stages that the death of a husband or wife transcends its immediate significance and assumes a greater, more profound meaning for the surviving spouse.

In learning to accept death we come to affirm life. In keeping with the tradition of the Old Testament we come to see the passing of a beloved spouse not as an irretrievable loss but as an accomplishment. It is not solely of a person's own making, but, as in the custom of the patriarchs, it is the fulfillment of a promise that if our partners in life have lived with integrity and faith they will be *remembered*. If they have kept the covenant that was given to them, demonstrating truthfulness, justice, and responsibility and inspiring us to do the same, the character of their lives will live on beyond them, even when they have been "gathered to their people" (see Gen. 25:8).

In the New Testament these qualities of life and the fulfillment of promise take on a more personal meaning in light of the resurrection. In the writings of Paul the meaning of death assumes its highest spiritual dimensions. Death is no longer considered a loss and is more than an accomplishment; it becomes a victory. In his letters to the early churches Paul addresses the issue of death, attempting to both understand and clarify its mystery. For Paul there is no meaning in death or purpose in life apart from faith in Jesus Christ. Death is a terrifying event for us; it is the end of our temporal existence, yet through God's redemptive work in the resurrection of Christ from the dead, our lives become imperishable and immortal. We dwell with Christ in eternal triumph over death, and the meaning and purpose of our lives as we have known them remain intact in life *after* death. Thus Paul makes the claim, "Death has been swallowed up in victory," and asks the triumphant question of death: "Where . . . is *your* victory? Where . . . is your sting?" (1 Cor. 15:54–55).

If you are facing or have already experienced the loss of your spouse to illness or disease you will want to remember the brightest and best about your mate, and you will want those memories to live forever. You may also want the assurance that because you knew your spouse's life to be so precious and unique, he or she must live on in greater accomplishment and triumph beyond the finality of death as we experience it. Life must have meaning and purpose as we live and share it together. It follows that meaning and purpose must also be found in death.

While I was in California doing research for this book, I took time away from my work to visit Yosemite National Park. I wanted to see the various rock formations I had heard about all my life, especially El Capitan, the largest single exposed piece of granite in the world. While driving around the park in search of it late one afternoon, I stopped to take a picture of the autumn foliage, thinking I was some distance from my intended goal and would not reach it before nightfall. As I turned around to walk back to my car, I happened to look up for some reason and suddenly there it was, El Capitan, rising before me, filling my eyes with its grandeur almost as far as I could see. I was transfixed; I stood there in awe and wonder, watching as the rays of the evening sun shone directly on its facade, giving it a brilliant and beautiful orange hue.

Several months later I had the occasion to tell of this experience during the funeral of one of our church members who had suddenly died of a heart attack while playing golf. Jay was a pillar of the church, and during the service I made the remark that pillars were not supposed to die. They should be like the rock El Capitan, standing forever as a sentinel overlooking the valley below, keeping watch over the trees and flowers that bloom and fade, the birds of the air that fly over the peaks, and even the people who come to the valley from generation to generation to behold its beauty. But we all know that even the greatest of rocks will crumble, and we are reminded, perhaps too often, that pillars in our church and in soci-

ety will die. So it is with the passing of a beloved husband
or wife, who was once our helpmate and confidant, who
held us up and sustained us during our life together. But
even as we mourn our loss we search for meaning in this
death because our mate was so important to us in life.
What does the death of a spouse mean to us? It means
that he or she has kept the faith and passed through
suffering with dignity and strength, having won a lasting
victory in our eyes as well as in God's. It means that we
rejoice for our beloved; we are inspired to demonstrate
in our lives those same qualities of integrity and resolve
that he or she showed. It means that we affirm life, here
and hereafter, knowing that our partner will not be forgotten. If we can understand and accept death in the
midst of our spouse's dying and our suffering in these
terms, then death *has* lost its sting—because life becomes all the more precious and eternal for us. Our
spouse who passed from our life will be remembered and
our loss becomes our gain—which is a great accomplishment and an even greater victory.

12

Faith, Hope, and Clarity

We began this book by referring to the onset of your spouse's illness or disease as a critical event. It was an incident in your lives together for which neither of you was adequately prepared.

By now your own experience as a caregiver may validate that claim. Your partner's critical or chronic illness has had a major, perhaps permanent, impact on the way you live and what you believe in. It has changed your identity as a marriage partner and recast your relationship with friends and other family members. It has challenged your basic values as an individual and probably called into question many of the things you once took for granted on a daily basis. Moreover, it may have significantly altered your socioeconomic situation.

On the assumption that your mate's illness has been *the* crisis event in your married life, I want to raise a final issue in our discussion of spousal support, an issue of ultimate meaning and concern.

What does your spouse's illness mean to you? What is its ultimate purpose? To what extent is the crisis event of illness in your spouse's life a faith event in your lives together?

This last chapter is called "Faith, Hope, and Clarity" on the strength of my conviction that every critical encounter in life is a matter of ultimate concern. Every event that produces lasting change must have lasting significance, and it is our right and responsibility to know what that is. Your spouse's illness has caused major changes in the form of pain, suffering, and emotional upheaval, and while its sudden occurrence makes no sense at all in your circumstances, you want to believe that there is a reason for the undue hardship you have faced since your husband or wife was taken sick. You want to have faith that the illness has some ultimate purpose, which you hope will become clear to you over time and in the course of your duties as a caregiver.

Faith

In its traditional Judeo-Christian interpretation, faith has always been regarded as the cornerstone of a disciplined life. Since the days of the Old Testament prophets it was understood that faith demanded obedience in all times, good and bad, and not to have faith was wrong because it would sow the seeds of doubt, which would crowd out faith when some future calamity occurred. It would follow in your case that the bad time you are having now with your spouse's illness could be misconstrued as a *loss* of a faith. Something is very wrong with your mate's health, and you lack the ability to understand or accept it as part of your life together. You have failed the test of faith, and the crucible of your partner's illness becomes a crisis of faith itself.

Faith is a necessary ingredient in coping with any crisis situation. Lack of faith is not an indication of guilt or a justification for punishment for feeling afraid or failing to understand the meaning of suffering in your life. Faith need not be a trial or a hindrance to what you believe, and it should serve as an additional source of support in helping you discover the purpose behind your spouse's illness or disease. Faith is a belief and trust in something beyond ourselves on which we depend for meaning and support. In the New Testament letter to the Hebrews, the writer describes faith as "the assurance of things hoped for, the conviction of things not seen" (Heb. 11:1). To have faith, then, is to trust in what we do not yet know for a fact and to believe in what we do not understand. In the case of your spouse's illness, you do not understand the reason behind it and you do not know what its ultimate end will be. But you want to have faith that meaning will come and the illness will end well.

It is this kind of dynamic, expectant faith that will support you in the course of your mate's critical or chronic illness. It is this kind of faith that is so amply demonstrated in people who have prevailed over illness and disease in their own lives together. Two such persons are Eddie and Evelyn Linnbaum. They have been married for fifty-five years, during which time Eddie has undergone eighty-three operations, for everything from a broken back just after his marriage, to numerous surgeries for cancer, to open heart surgery in 1988. In all the years and the medical crises they have weathered together, Eddie and Evelyn have remained committed to each other and steadfast in their faith that God would see them through. I interviewed them both specifically for this book and asked Evelyn as a veteran caregiver how her faith had supported her while she supported her husband in the many illnesses, critical and chronic, that he has endured throughout their married life. She replied, "You need to be strong and keep going. I think God expects that. And you have to draw your strength from one another. God helps both of us when we are together."

Evelyn described a particular experience in which her faith literally helped them both get through the night together.

> I was walking around the house with Eddie all night before he went to the hospital for lung cancer surgery. We were trying to convince each other that he would be all right. . . . I kept praying for Eddie, but I couldn't concentrate. . . . I just felt worse until I

realized that my mind was really drifting to where
God could tell us that even if Eddie didn't get well
this time God would still take care of us.

Evelyn had a difficult and frustrating night in facing up
to Eddie's illness until her faith began to work for her.
She interpreted the experience this way:

You ask God for something in a bad situation to make
you feel better. Then he leads you somewhere else
and gives you what you need and leads you back to
where you were, and you know your prayers were
answered. It's like your mind was led astray for a
while until you realize that God is taking charge of
your life and will work everything out for your own
good according to his plan.

Evelyn believed she could trust God to care for her when
she was afraid, just as she knew Eddie could trust her to
care for him when he was sick. That was a real act of faith.
Evelyn could reach beyond her own fear and limitations
and be led to understand that her husband's illness had
some purpose in God's plan for their life together.

This is the kind of faith that gets us through the crises
of serious illness and disease. It is vibrant and alive. It
gives meaning to our present circumstances and promises that our suffering and anguish will work to our ultimate good. Of course, this kind of faith is not without its
legitimate doubts. It is not easy to be assured of what you
do not know or have not seen, especially when that applies to critical and chronic illness. Evelyn herself has
experienced the conflict of doubt versus faith in her role
as a caregiving wife. During our interview she recounted
the feelings she had during Eddie's open heart surgery.

I'll never forget it when they told me he could die
on the operating table or if he lived he might never
be the same again. I was praying for a miracle that
he would recover like he always did. Who would I
believe in now, God or the doctors? I had to trust in

God. I was so afraid that there was nowhere else to go.

Evelyn describes what many of us have learned from our caregiving experience. Faith, real faith, works when it is needed the most—in times of personal doubt and despair. Faith without doubt, however, may not work at all. Faith apart from individual experience is basically untested, because we have yet fully to apply or utilize it to our own advantage in understanding the reason for our spouse's illness.

As a caregiving spouse you want to know why your husband or wife suffered a heart attack or fell victim to cancer, and you want to believe that he or she will recover. You want this whole painful experience to make sense to you, and you want it to end well. But you do not know right now that it will. Significant doubt remains. You question your faith. What can you do to keep it intact? How can you overcome your conflict?

I believe you can only overcome it by taking a risk, a risk on the side of faith versus doubt. I call your attention again to the simple yet profound observation of Paul Tillich that doubt is overcome by a "leap" of faith. A leap always involves risk, and when you leap or dive headlong into the uncertainty of your partner's illness you are risking the possibility of learning that he or she will never get well and never knowing why, but you are also affirming your belief that even in the midst of doubt and uncertainty you will prevail. You will continue to care for your mate because you trust and believe that God will continue to care for you.

Taking a leap of faith in the midst of your spouse's critical or chronic illness is a real act of commitment. It demands risk and may result in great personal disappointment. But bear in mind that it can also lead to a whole new source of support in your life as a caregiver and to a new level of trust and assurance that God will not only care for you but will show you something of the mystery behind your spouse's illness that you could never see before. This is the way faith works. It reveals knowledge. It inspires truth and it is inexhaustible. In the course of my conversation with the Linnbaums, Eddie expressed his own thoughts on what faith was and how it worked for him.

> You have to let go and let God be and do what he wants. . . . You have to believe like Noah or Job that doing something ridiculous in people's eyes—because God said to—makes sense. They all said I wouldn't survive the heart surgery, and I was sitting up in my bed the next morning drinking coffee. . . . We've always known that with God's help I would get better, and I have every time. God has never failed us, no matter how sick I've been.

When it comes to faith, Eddie speaks very well for all of us.

Hope

As you search for lasting meaning within your spouse's illness or disease through the power of your faith, you hope that meaning will come. Hope is the confidence that faith inspires. Hope issues from faith; it is the expectation that faith's intent will be fulfilled. In the letter to the Romans, the apostle Paul portrays hope as an instrument of rescue: "For in hope we were saved. Now hope that is seen is not hope. For who hopes for what is seen? But if we hope for what we do not see, we wait for it with patience" (Rom. 8:24–25). The rescue is certain but not immediate; it is sight unseen, and we must wait for its final disclosure with patience.

In the occurrence of critical illness and disease, hope is that impulse that frees us from the darkness and despair we feel over the prospect of endless caring for our spouse in the future. It leads to the belief that our spouse's illness will amount to something positive because we have tried to do our best in providing spousal support. To care as much as we can for our partners and to hope that we will eventually learn what the illness means for our lives together—even as we wait for our deliverance from the burden of caring—is an awesome task, but that is what we do as caregivers.

Alice is a caregiving wife to her husband, Carl, who suffered a stroke in 1987. She saw my request for information on caring for disabled spouses in a local stroke organization newsletter and responded by sending me her diary for a whole year! In it she gives an honest and detailed account of her own experience in caring for her husband. Of particular significance is how Alice hopes for the best possible outcome in her situation, while coping with her feelings of hopelessness, despair, and anger.

Alice begins on a positive note by including a verse in her diary from a poem she read about building a "strong box" in which to keep your troubles. Her diary is her "strong box." Alice hopes that expressing herself in writing will help her cope with her husband's condition.

> Since my feelings sometimes get the best of me I thought I'd explain them in this journal. . . . It's been two years this month since Carl's "accident," and with all that I have had to do I need a place to go for support myself. . . .
>
> I've tried this writing and it's very helpful—it's like talking to a friend who never leaves and really listens! I hope the effect doesn't wear off and I can keep on caring for Carl the way he needs.

Alice hopes for the best from her journal experience— the inspiration and support she needs for herself in order to provide the kind of care her husband needs as a stroke victim. Yet in the course of her writing she encounters other, less confident feelings, feelings which, as she says, "keep coming out of the strong box."

In contrast to hope, Alice feels hopelessness and despair. The burden of care that she must assume for her husband is pointless and overwhelming. She is exhausted and wonders how she can go on.

> I really don't know how I'll get through this. I am so tired tonight. I fall asleep in the chair just like the old woman I have become. . . . There is no reason for life anymore, and I'm getting so tired of trying to find one. . . . Why do I keep hoping for better things? I should just hope for nothing worse, like my mother used to tell me.

In her depression and despair, Alice is willing just to settle for things as they are. Experience has taught her a painful lesson: life will not improve. She will even listen to her mother's past admonitions that she be grateful for the status quo and hope that things will not deteriorate further—that Carl will not have another stroke, and her caregiving duties will not increase.

In addition to despairing over her situation, Alice is also angry about it. In her own defense she looks for a way out of her new life as a caregiving spouse even as she tries to accept it, but she realizes the anger and resentment are still there.

> I have always been bitter over these changes in my life. I thought I could get over that by convincing myself things were normal again, but my anger keeps coming back. . . . I pray for strength to get through these years, but I don't think my prayers are getting through, or maybe God doesn't *listen*. . . . I don't know how others do it. How can they live with a stroke victim? Surely I'm not the only one who is so damned to nothing. How do I accept this living death? *Why* should I?

Alice is angry because she has lost control of her life. She can no longer deny her feelings as she explores the causes for her resentment. Alice is angry at God because God is not answering her prayers for strength to make her life normal again. She is resentful of others whom she perceives as living successfully with the effects of stroke. Alice is most angry, however, with her husband, the "stroke victim" whose life she shares and whose illness she sees as a virtual condemnation of her whole existence. There is no life for her apart from Carl's illness, and she is very angry.

How can Alice find hope in her life as a caregiving spouse when her conflicting feelings of anger and despair are so sensitive and strong? How can she find that message of inspiration and support to care for Carl and live with his limitations successfully?

The answer for Alice, as with all of us who are faced with this same question as caregiver, is to have hope, which is to say that we *rediscover* the hope that lies within us. When we realize what we already have to do our jobs well, our chances for success are more assured. When we care for our disabled spouses we have hope for success, but we have it in smaller doses and look for smaller successes. When we lower our expectations in our jobs as caregiving spouses we diminish our anger and despair so our hopes can be fulfilled.

Alice's hopes for Carl were fulfilled when she learned to lower her expectations for his progress and recovery from his stroke. Toward the end of her diary she writes about an evening when Carl went out for the first time without her to a Masonic lodge meeting. He wanted to go, and Alice made the arrangements for his being picked up and returned home. While he was gone, Alice worried constantly. "Would he be all right?" she wondered. "Would everyone be kind to him? Would he make it?" We pick up on Alice's journal entry that day marked 9:30 P.M., after which she wrote:

> He's home! He survived and I survived. He brought home a pin, a program, and lemon pie all over his shirt, but he's beaming and I am so proud. It was a good thing to let him go—I wondered if I should have—but it was good. It was a good day to keep out

of the "strong box"—there was no need to hide this day! Now try not to worry about tomorrow!

Alice hoped Carl would be all right that evening—that he would make it. That was all she hoped for: making it to and from his lodge meeting. In this instance, Alice got what she hoped for—a little display of Carl's independence. It was a small success, but it gave a great reward to Alice. She was beaming too. She felt good about caring for her husband again, and her feelings of anger and despair went away for a while.

Alice rediscovered the hope she always had that her husband could improve further in his recovery from stroke—even if it was in smaller doses. Through that discovery she found new and lasting meaning in Carl's illness and in her role as a caregiving wife. As a caregiving spouse you can have the same experience—if you have hope. You can find lasting significance in the small successes your partner achieves in recovery from critical or chronic illness, whether it is a night out alone, using the telephone correctly, or even getting out of bed unassisted for the first time. Rediscover that hope which lies within you as part of your faith in God. It will save you from the anger and despair that can cripple your life as a caregiver even more than the effects of your spouse's illness. Look for hope. If you do not yet see it, wait for it with patience and it will come, where and when you least expect it—at a time and place of God's own choosing.

Clarity

As you continue to care for your husband or wife and seek out the meaning behind this illness, the need for clarity becomes more apparent. The longer you are involved in the process of caring, the more you need to know about why you are doing it. It is only through a further understanding of the cause and effects of your partner's illness that its full meaning becomes clear.

In your search for the meaning of your spouse's illness or disease you will encounter your share of ambiguity and confusion. Pursuing knowledge in anything is always a confusing task because you are never quite sure what you are looking for until you find it. Yet you go on believing that at some point what you do not know will be revealed to you. It is a dilemma that Paul describes to the members of the church at Corinth: "For now we see in a mirror, dimly, but then we will see face to face. Now I know only in part; then I will know fully, even as I have been fully known." (1 Cor. 13:12).

How do you find clarity in your continuing life as a caregiving spouse? How will your faith help you live with what you do not know about your partner's illness now, and how will you hope to understand it in the future?

Being clear about your spouse's illness means that you first understand its cause. What made it happen? Who made it happen? Was it an accident, a twist of fate? Did God make it happen? If it was an accident, who do you blame? If it was not, how do you blame God?

Placing blame is a first step in understanding the reason for your spouse's illness or disease. Like the early stages of the grief process described in chapter 2, it is an emotional reaction to suffering which allows us eventually to understand and accept our spouse's illness and deal with it on a more rational basis.

I tried to place blame when I was looking for the cause of my wife's illness. As a Christian I did not see her stroke as an accident or an act of fate. I saw it clearly as an act of God, and I blamed God for taking Jackie away from me. However, I could not ultimately believe that the God whom I loved—and believed loved me and Jackie— could do such a thing. It was contrary to my sense of reason and my faith. I did not believe in fate and I could no longer blame God. So there I was with nowhere to go in my search for understanding the cause of Jackie's illness.

Eventually it became clear to me that my wife's stroke

was neither God's fault nor an accident. I came to see that it was the result of evil. I confess to being too much of a twentieth-century man to believe in a personal power of evil in the world such as Lucifer or the devil, but I do believe in evil as an intelligent, malevolent force. I believe it comes at will to threaten and destroy us, and we are always at risk. I believe the power of evil caused Jackie's stroke.

I also believe in the redemptive power of God. By redemptive power I mean that God can change things for the better. God takes the power of evil and turns it into good. I am convinced that God did that with my wife's illness when she awoke from her coma and recovered from her stroke.

As you search for the deeper significance within your spouse's illness or disease, you may want to attribute its cause to a wide array of sources. You may believe God did it, you may be convinced the devil did it, or you may know for a fact who did it. Regardless of its source, however, I believe its cause can be clarified and understood and your partner's illness can be redeemed. I am convinced that God can help you make sense out of the reason your husband or wife became ill and can change the suffering that you experience as a caregiving spouse into healing and wholeness. You begin by accepting the cause as just, and you go on believing that it will end in a deeper, more meaningful and loving relationship with your spouse in the future.

A deeper and more meaningful relationship with your husband or wife produces some lasting effects. It makes you more acceptable to each other—even under the most trying circumstances of giving and receiving care. It acknowledges that trying times will be the norm and not the exception in your life together and that "normalcy" as you once perceived it is largely a myth. It helps you accept change, not as a detriment in your life but as a challenge to learn new ideas and skills and discover new opportunities for continued growth and happiness

in your future. Finally, a deeper, more loving relationship with your mate finds its highest expression in your
relationship with God. God brings redemption and
wholeness into your lives; you see it more clearly every
day you live, work, and grow in harmony together. There
is a balance of body, mind, and soul in your own life as
well. God loves you, and now you know it fully even as
you are known, and that makes you feel glad to be alive.

This feeling was expressed very well in a letter I received from a caregiving wife in Canada who wrote to
me about the first time her husband greeted her in the
hospital after months of therapy by standing up from his
wheelchair to hug and kiss her. Tears came to her eyes
when he spoke his first sentence: "Isn't life beautiful?"
She replied, "It is, and it always will be." I doubt that any
of us could say it any better.

And, Finally, Love

This chapter opened with the assertion that every critical event in life is a matter of ultimate concern and we
have the rightful task to discover its ultimate significance
for ourselves. We have explored how, in the event of
critical illness and disease, ultimate significance is found
in terms of faith, hope, and clarity.

Faith is the starting point of discovering the significance of anything. You must first believe there is significance in something and then believe you can find it.
Does your spouse's illness mean anything to you? Surely
it means a great deal. Do you believe you can find that
meaning for yourself? You can and you will if its discovery is as critical to you as finding a cure for your spouse's
illness is to your spouse. Real faith works best in crisis.
Sometimes it works wonders; sometimes it works miracles.

In the darkest days of my wife's illness, I made a pastoral call on an old friend and member of my church, Norm
Taylor, who was suffering from terminal cancer. He had

been away at the time of Jackie's stroke and had written me a beautiful letter in which he expressed his deep distress about Jackie's condition and his complete confidence that she would recover. The letter was remarkable, since his own condition was rapidly deteriorating and he knew he would not live. He wrote, "I was shocked to hear of Jackie's sudden illness. . . . She is constantly in my thoughts and central in my frequent prayers. . . . I believe that Jackie will have a quick and full recovery and that our faith will not be shaken." Norm also wrote that he had "great faith in the power of individual prayer," and when we sat down to pray together at his home that day he asked if he could pray first. In his prayer Norm asked God for what he believed in, Jackie's quick and complete recovery. He asked nothing for himself. Within a few weeks Jackie woke up and began to recover from her stroke. Within a few months my old friend died.

I have always recalled those moments spent with Norm as a time of great discovery for me, a time in which I found an example of inspiring faith that soared above the crises of the moment, his and mine. It was a wonder to me that Norm could pray so confidently for Jackie's life when he knew that he would die and I believed that Jackie would also. It was, and still is, a miracle that his prayers were answered and Jackie beat the overwhelming odds against her to survive her illness. It has always been a matter of personal loss to me that my prayers for Norm were not answered as I asked. I often wonder if my faith was strong enough for him.

Real faith, personal faith, can overcome any crisis in our lives. It can overcome the critical, chronic, or even terminal illness in your spouse's life. It can inspire you to rise above it and discover its true meaning and intent as a matter of ultimate concern. Real faith is power. It is your possession of the infinite and miraculous power of God to redeem your life and give it back to you so that you will win the day and turn any tragedy into certain triumph. This is the way faith works. This is what happens when you have faith.

Hope is the means and manifestation of faith. When you have hope you know faith is working. Hope conducts faith from its source to its object. The source of your faith is God. The object of faith is your spouse's recovery from illness. It is through hope that your objective is met. You hope for your spouse's return to health; you hope for the best.

Hope does not guarantee, however, that your objective will be met. It does not assure success in every adverse condition of life. It only provides the ways and means for faith to be fulfilled. The writer of the psalms knows this well as he calls upon God in the hope of his deliverance from despair:

> Out of the depths I cry to you, O Lord.
>   Lord, hear my voice!
> I wait for the Lord, my soul waits,
>   and in his word I hope;
> For with the Lord there is steadfast love,
>   and with him is great power to redeem.
>   Psalm 130:1–2, 5, 7

Hope requires waiting, but the object of hope is worth waiting for. This is the purpose of having hope in the depths of tears and despair. It leads to the redeeming love of God, which is both absolute and overabundant. This is the ultimate end of hope for the psalmist. In the course of your spouse's illness, it is the ultimate end of hope for you. The illness may end with your partner's return to health or it may not, but you may be assured all along the way that God will be a constant source of support to you as you support your spouse. This is what hope is. This is what it means to have it and hope for the best.

Clarity is seeing what you believe in. In the words of an old Protestant hymn, it is "faith's fair vision changing into sight." Clarity follows faith and hope when the object of faith is fully known and the ends of hope are fully achieved. When the ultimate significance of your spouse's illness becomes clear, you discover what the meaning of that illness really is for you and why you continue to care as you do. In my own life I care for and about Jackie more than I ever thought I would because I believe that God literally woke her up. I see the ultimate purpose of her illness as a witness to God's grace and redemption and an opportunity for us to tell a wonderful story of the triumph of good over evil. You may understand your spouse's illness and why you care in less dramatic but equally important ways. It may be that your husband's heart attack has caused a change in lifestyle that will ultimately add years to his life instead of taking them away, and the time you have left together promises to be richer and fuller than you ever thought possible. Perhaps your wife's experience with cancer has left you shaken but much more sensitive to her suffering and willing to care for her needs in the future.

The ultimate significance of your spouse's illness is what you discover and make it out to be. It is believing in what you see and acting on that belief. It is acting on good faith to make life better and your marriage happier. It is to affirm that, even in the worst possible circumstances of your life, good can and will come out of evil.

Clarity also leads you to discover new levels of learning and awareness, beyond the immediate circumstances of your spouse's illness and your life as a caregiver, that you can apply to other times and places in your life. Through Jackie's illness I learned more about love. I knew I loved Jackie and God loved me, but what I did not know was how long-suffering love could be. I learned from personal faith and experience what I always read that love "bears all things, believes all things . . . endures all things" (1 Cor. 13:7). I learned that love can outlast anything and is, in fact, the one thing that still stands when everything else falls all around me and I have nothing else left. I also learned that the ultimate meaning of love is to give and not to receive, and that with love I could give up anything because love "does not insist on its own way. . . . Love never ends" (1 Cor. 13:5, 8). Even as I gave up my insistence on Jackie's return to health and placed her life in God's hands, I realized her life would go on for some greater purpose in the mind of God and I would continue to love her still.

If you are clear on what your spouse's illness ultimately means in your life, you have learned about love also. You know God loves you and you have learned to love your husband or wife without question and with total acceptance. You have come to love your mate as you yourself have always wanted to be loved and as God has always loved you.

You have become aware of God's grace in your life and what it truly means to care. To care means that to some extent you see yourself in other people. This is grace. It is the God-given capacity to understand and accept those whom we love in the sense that we are a part of them and all that happens in their lives.

This is what it means to be married to someone who is critically or chronically ill. It is to understand and accept your husband or wife in the midst of pain and make the pain part of your own. It is to share in his or her suffering so that he or she may share in your strength. It is, as a matter of ultimate concern, to stand up with your spouse before the presence of evil and the threat of destruction, knowing that as you stand together God goes before you to save and deliver you into God's care—which never fails and never ends because God loves you and will never let you go.

Resources

Books

Cole, Harry A. *The Long Way Home: Spiritual Help When Someone You Love Has a Stroke.* Louisville, Ky.: Westminster/John Knox Press, 1989.

———— and Martha M. Jablow. *One in a Million.* Boston: Little, Brown & Co., 1990.

Dass, Ram, and Paul Gorman. *How Can I Help?* New York: Alfred A. Knopf, 1987.

Friedman, Jo-Ann. *Home Health Care: A Complete Guide for Patients and Their Families.* New York: W. W. Norton & Co., 1986.

Horne, Jo. *Helping an Aged Loved One.* Washington, D.C.: American Association of Retired Persons, 1985.

How to Hire Helpers. Seattle: Task Force on Aging, Church Council of Greater Seattle (4759 15th Street NE, Seattle, WA 98105), n.d.

Jeffers, Susan. *Feel the Fear and Do It Anyway.* San Diego: Harcourt Brace Jovanovich, 1987.

Kubler-Ross, Elisabeth. *On Death and Dying.* New York: Macmillan Co., 1969.

Kushner, Harold S. *When All You've Ever Wanted Isn't Enough.* New York: Summit Books, 1986.

————. *When Bad Things Happen to Good People.* New York: Schocken Books, 1981.

Mace, Nancy L., and Peter V. Rabins. *The Thirty-Six*

Hour Day: A Family Guide to Caring for Persons with Alzheimer's Disease, Related Dementing Illnesses, and Memory Loss in Later Life. Baltimore: Johns Hopkins University Press, 1982.

Murphey, Cecil. *Day by Day: Spiritual Help When Someone You Love Has Alzheimer's*. Louisville, Ky.: Westminster/John Knox Press, 1988.

Salisbury, Christine L., and James Intagliata, eds. *Respite Care: Support for Persons with Developmental Disabilities and Their Families*. Baltimore: Paul H. Brookes Publishing Co., 1986.

Schmidt, Stephen A. *Living with Chronic Illness*. Minneapolis: Augsburg Publishing House, 1989.

Siegel, Bernie S. *Love, Medicine and Miracles*. New York: Harper & Row, 1986.

Veninga, Robert L. *A Gift of Hope: How We Survive Our Tragedies*. Boston: Little, Brown & Co., 1986.

Viorst, Judith. *Necessary Losses*. New York: Simon & Schuster, 1986.

Organizations

American Cancer Society
261 Madison Avenue
New York, NY 10016

American Diabetes Association
1660 Duke Street
Alexandria, VA 22313

American Heart Association
7320 Greenville Avenue
Dallas, TX 75231

Lupus Foundation of America
1717 Massachusetts Avenue., NW, Suite 203
Washington, D.C. 20036

National Association of People with AIDS
2025 I Street NW, Suite 415
Washington, DC 20006

National Head Injury Foundation
333 Turnpike Road
Southborough, MA 01772

National Multiple Sclerosis Society
205 East 42nd Street
New York, NY 10017

National Stroke Association
300 East Hampden Avenue, Suite 240
Englewood, CO 80110-2622

National Well Spouse Foundation
Box 2878
San Diego, CA 92198-0876

Sample Documents

Living wills and durable powers of attorney for health vary from state to state. The following samples are generic in form and are not intended to be legally binding. You may obtain your state's version of living will laws from your State Attorney General's office or from the Society for the Right to Die, 250 East 57th Street, New York, NY 10107.

Living Will Declaration

To My Family, Doctors, and All Those Concerned with My Care

I, _____, being of sound mind, make this statement as a directive to be followed if I become unable to participate in decisions regarding my medical care.

If I should be in an incurable or irreversible mental or physical condition with no reasonable expectation of recovery, I direct my attending physician to withhold or withdraw treatment that merely prolongs my dying. I further direct that treatment be limited to measures to keep me comfortable and to relieve pain.

These directions express my legal right to refuse treatment. Therefore, I expect my family, doctors, and everyone concerned with my care to regard themselves as legally and morally bound to act in accord with my wishes, and in so doing to be free of any legal liability for having followed my directions.

I especially do not want: _____

_____

_____

Other instructions/comments: _____

_____

Proxy Designation Clause: Should I become unable to communicate my instructions as stated above, I designate the following person to act in my behalf:

Name _____

Address _____

If the person I have named above is unable to act in my behalf, I authorize the following person to do so:

Name _____

Address _____

Signed:_____Date: _____

Witness:_____Witness:_____

Keep the signed original with your personal papers at home. Give signed copies to doctors, family, and proxy. Review your declaration from time to time; initial and date it to show it still expresses your wishes.

Durable Power of Attorney

I hereby designate _____ to serve as my attorney-in-fact for purpose of making medical decisions. This power of attorney shall remain in effect in the event that I become incompetent or otherwise unable to make such decisions for myself.

Optional Notarization:

Sworn and subscribed to before me this _____ day of _____, 19___.

Signed _____

Date _____

Witness _____

_____
Notary Public
(seal)

_____
Address

Witness _____

_____

Copies of this request have been given to

_____

_____